Jake

to P. J. Edington

Happy Anniversary
you and Will are
great friends.
Thanks

Oct 1991

Jake Pickle

JAKE

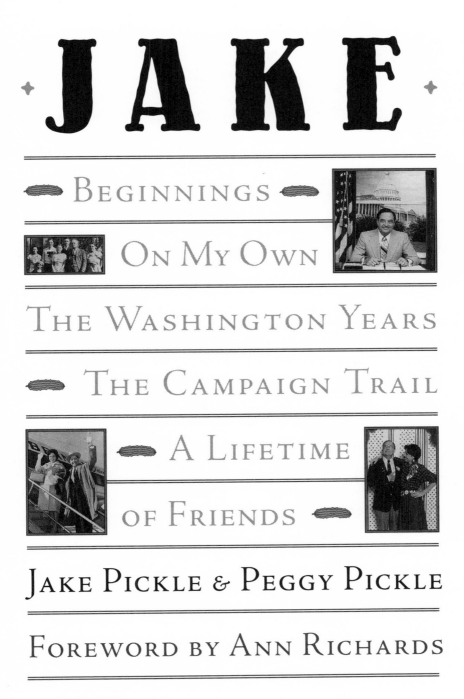

BEGINNINGS

ON MY OWN

THE WASHINGTON YEARS

THE CAMPAIGN TRAIL

A LIFETIME

OF FRIENDS

JAKE PICKLE & PEGGY PICKLE

FOREWORD BY ANN RICHARDS

UNIVERSITY OF TEXAS PRESS   AUSTIN

First edition, 1997

Requests for permission to reproduce material from this work should be sent
to Permissions, University of Texas Press, Box 7819, Austin, TX 78713-7819.

∞

The paper used in this publication meets the minimum requirements of
American National Standard for Information Sciences—Permanence of
Paper for Printed Library Materials, ANSI Z39.48-1984

LIBRARY OF CONGRESS CATALOGING-IN-PUBLICATION DATA

Pickle, J. J.
Jake / by Jake Pickle and Peggy Pickle ; foreword by Ann Richards. — 1st ed.
p.   cm.
Includes index.
ISBN 0-292-76572-X (alk. paper).
1. Pickle, J. J.   2. Legislators—United States—Biography.
3. United States. Congress. House—Biography.   4. Texas—Politics
and government—1951–   I. Pickle, Peggy, date.   II. Title.
E840.8.P53A3   1997
328.73'092—dc20   96-10090

Designed by Ellen McKie

Contents

Ann Richards

Foreword

In World War II, young men inducted, outfitted, and turned into officers almost overnight were called ninety-day wonders. My friend Jake Pickle started his public service back then, but he is well on his way to becoming a ninety-*year* wonder—a man whose public spirit and commitment to service continue at a time in life when most of us are more worried about the state of our mind than the state of the union.

You do not hear about it as much now, but in Jake's youth and my youth, tremendous value was placed on what was called *personality*. For some people, that word conjures up the image of a friend pitching the virtues of a blind date and intoning, "He's not much to look at, but he has a great personality." But in another era, the word meant more; it was about manner and how you carried yourself and your instincts about other people. Personality had to do with being personable, but it also had to do with being able to bring other people into the flow of what you were doing—whether you were telling a joke or running for office. It could not be learned, but it was, for those who had it, effortless.

In that older Texas sense of the word, Jake has personality. That means he is something that is rare even in Texas: Jake is a political natural.

Even so, Jake and I started out on opposite sides of the political fence. When I was a college student—and totally confident that I had a corner on political wisdom and rectitude—I was a dyed-in-the-wood supporter of Ralph Yarborough and Jake Pickle was a key aide to Governor Allan Shivers. If you know the Texas politics of that era, you know that emotions ran high and grudges lasted long. There are still Texans of a certain age who can allow a discussion of the 1956 Democratic convention to degenerate into blows.

So it tells you a lot about Jake Pickle to know that thirty years later, when his re-election was challenged by a well-known local politician, he had a fund-raiser that looked like a reunion of all sides from that 1956 convention. And if there was any anger at that event, it was directed squarely at his challenger. By 1986, running against Jake was regarded by liberals, conservatives, and middle-of-the-roaders as ridiculous and rude.

Jake won that election with 72 percent of the vote. Publicly, he was delighted. Privately, he probably thought he should have campaigned harder for that other 28 percent—which goes a long way toward explaining Jake's success. He always thought he was in a world of trouble if he got less than 70 percent of the vote.

When Braniff Airlines flew direct from Washington to Austin, Jake was legendary for working the aisle—shaking hands with every passenger on board. If you got on that airplane with Jake, you were not getting off until he had called you by name and asked what he could do for you.

That refusal to let an opportunity pass is part of the Pickle work ethic. For Jake, early to rise and early to work are simply the price of admission, the opening ante for the game.

During one campaign, Jake and I were out block-walking a university neighborhood around nine in the morning. We rang a doorbell at one house a couple of times with no answer. We were about to leave a piece of literature and walk away when the door opened. The householder was a young man who greeted us dripping wet with a towel wrapped around his lower half. As I recall, he was a rather attractive young man.

Jake started as if he were going to do the regular drill. "Good morning," he said. "I'm your Congressman, Jake Pickle, and I'm running for re-election."

But then you could tell he just could not stand to let it go.

"Say," he asked, "did you just get up?"

And the young man said, well, as a matter of fact, he had not been awake very long.

Jake, who always sprinkles his conversation liberally with "Lyndon would have said," locked in eye-to-eye on that young man, took on the tone of a Dutch uncle, and said, "Well, son, like Lyndon would have said, I hope you know that every man in Austin got a head start on you this morning."

Thrift is one of Jake's virtues, too. He is the first to attribute a good part of his accomplishments to the fact that he is cheap. I suspect that one reason he was such a good member of Congress is that his tightness with the personal purse strings translated well to the stewardship of public dollars. And his campaigns always felt the Pickle penny-pinch.

When I was governor and, as such, could draw a pretty decent crowd, Jake decided that there was no reason why I could not march in a parade and help his campaign at the same time. We were going to the Luling Watermelon Thump, and Jake brought along a supply of those green plastic whistles shaped like pickles that he gives away. He handed me a bag of the pickles with the instruction that I was to throw them to kids on the parade route. I was enthusiastic about my task. So it was not long before I had exhausted my pickle supply, and I ran back to Jake to get more.

Jake looked at me as if he could not believe what he was seeing and said, "Surely you haven't given them all out! Those things cost twenty-three cents apiece!"

And when I said that, well, they were real popular with the kids, Jake said, "Listen, when I started out, I could buy those whistles for six cents each, but that doesn't mean everyone who wanted one could have one. You can't let those kids take advantage of you that way."

Jake could afford to be tight with a dollar because he was always generous with himself. He and Beryl made time for the kids but, beyond that, their lives were given almost totally to public service. Jake worked long hours in Washington and came home often.

There's an old Texas political saying that holds, "You dance with them that brung you." Jake may have increased his power and influence in the Capitol every year, but he never forgot who brought him to the party. The people of the Tenth Congressional District were always his first concern. Jake was not born in Austin, but he embodies the Austin High School motto of "Loyal Forever."

He has made it clear that he likes his constituents and always has time for them. They have responded by treating him like what he is: home folks.

Years ago, I was attending the opening of the Manchaca Volunteer Fire Department's new building. I was seated with the dignitaries—on hay bales on the back of a flatbed truck. We were almost ready to start the ceremony when a big limousine pulled up and out of it came Speaker of the House Tip O'Neill and Majority Leader Jim Wright, followed by Jake.

One of the volunteer firefighters next to me turned to another and said, "Who is that big guy with the white hair?"

The other one replied, "I don't know who those guys are; must be friends of Jake."

When your world is as large as the local community, the speaker and the majority leader of the United States House of Representatives have next to no significance. What mattered was that they were with Jake, which meant they could be trusted. Besides, the speculation was true; they *were* friends of Jake, and so was everyone else. After thirty years in public office and more than fifty years in politics, the bottom line on Jake is that he has more friends, more support, and more credibility than he had when he started.

At John Connally's funeral, I was sitting in the fourth or fifth row and, as the service was getting started, a tardy Richard Nixon slid into the pew beside me. We exchanged pleasantries and he sat there silently surveying the crowd until he stopped on a face and said, more or less to himself, "My God, there's Jake Pickle!" It was as if he was surprised that Jake was still around. The irony was that not only was Jake still around, he was a living monument to what Richard Nixon so wanted but never achieved: the trust and affection of the public.

Jake has served his state and his country, but most of all he has rendered remarkable service to the people of the Tenth Congressional District. And no one ever did more in Washington for his beloved University of Texas. The robust economy that the Central Texas region now enjoys is in no small part the result of Jake's efforts to secure funding for the research, teaching, and technology development that have made the university a national and international leader.

Here in Austin and everywhere in the Hill Country, we are friends of Jake, and we are all profoundly grateful for what his friendship and public service have meant to us.

A.R.

Acknowledgments

I could not have accomplished any of the things described in this book without the support my family has given me. The last chapter, "Family Talent," attempts to describe that support. In addition, I would like to thank my nephew Gary Pickle and his wife Jan, nephew David Lancaster and his wife Cathy, and in-laws Missy McCarroll, Marsha McCarroll, Don Cook, Frances and Walter Bentson, Lois and Bill Wyatt, and Bunny and Ray Beall.

I appreciate Judge Homer Thornberry, Bess Jones, and Dan Rather sharing their stories and giving me permission to include them in this book.

Special thanks to former committee staffers Joe Grant, Janice Gregory, and Beth Vance, and David Koitz with the Congressional Research Service for their assistance on the legislative chapters.

And a salute to the late Bob Mueller, on whose loyal friendship and sound advice I depended for fifty years.

J.P.

Introduction

My father always said he'd never write a book.

He *still* says he hasn't written a book. He says we've compiled a *collection*: a collection of stories.

He loves political stories—especially his own—so this is OK with him. The thing he loves best about political stories is telling them. He never met an audience he didn't like—and I've never met an audience that didn't like his stories.

When he and I set out to write this *collection*, we had similar, yet separate goals. He wanted to preserve his favorite political stories. He believes there's more entertainment, drama, embarrassment, and escape in a good American political story than in any other form of national humor. Why? Because politicians are just as human as anybody else—but more inclined to get into impossible situations, more desperate to squirm out of them, and faster with a quip.

Each generation of politicians has its own brand of stories. As the political landscape changes, often these stories are forgotten. In writing this book, my father wants to make sure that some of *his* stories are not forgotten.

Like him, I wanted to preserve the stories, but I had another goal, too. I wanted to preserve the way my father conducted his Congressional career, because it seems to me that his was a kinder, more responsive attitude than exists in politics today. Despite differences, he treated political opponents with respect, and never held a grudge. He works harder—even in retirement—than anybody I know.

Growing up in a political family, I learned The Rules early, not because he preached them, but because he lived them. At first, I thought we should write about The Rules, sort of a "how to" book for aspiring politicians.

Briefly, some of Jake's rules are:

In a parade, don't get behind the horses!

. . . but do ride in a convertible with your name on the side.

Always be available to constituents.

Don't assume "they" won't find out about it, because they will.

If it doesn't pass "the smell test," don't do it.

A politician who expects financial privacy is in the wrong line of work.

Don't arrive at events too early, because they don't know what to do with you.

Listen for the bell.

Answer every constituent's letter within three days of its receipt.

If you don't know where the money came from, give it back.

Holding a drink gets in the way of shaking hands.

When you're in your home district, you can't say "No."

In a restaurant, face the door, so people can see and talk to you.

Always carry a pen and paper.

Introduce yourself first.

At barbecues, stand at the head of the food line; everybody has to pass by, and you get to shake their hand.

Never take it all for granted.

When I first approached my father in the summer of 1994 about writing a book, he was hesitant. He didn't want to fall into the familiar trap of a public figure self-importantly writing a memoir about his career—a memoir nobody really wants to read.

Several months later, when we knew he wasn't going to run for re-election, he agreed to think about a book. But he was adamant about not writing an autobiography, and he insisted we put off starting until he retired and "came home for good." The date of his retirement was January 1995.

But 1995 came, and for the first five months he was too busy—busy unpacking, setting up a new office, speaking to civic groups, returning to Washington to testify before Congressional committees. Anything but working on a book! He kept putting me off, saying, "Not now. Maybe next week."

Finally he committed to a date in May 1995. However, suddenly a much-loved member of his staff died. Instead of working on our book that day, he delivered a moving eulogy at his friend's funeral. We scheduled another date in June.

But when *that* day arrived, he appeared at my front door and said we would have to postpone it again: Vice President Al Gore was in town. He was meeting the Vice President in two hours. "I'll try to set up a time next week," he said.

But by now I had figured out there might never be a "good" time. I said, "We have two hours. Sit down." I even gave him a little push toward the easy chair I had set up beside my computer. So he sat, looking at his watch and telling me he wasn't used to working this way. But he began talking—and once he began, he got into the story. Which reminded him of *another* story . . .

That's how we started.

Over the next six months, he talked and I typed. He was used to dictating; I was used to composing directly into a word processor. We compromised. As he reminisced, I typed the details into my computer as fast as I could, stopping to ask questions. He *hated* when I did that! He'd be laughing about one of Pa Ferguson's speeches and all of a sudden I would pipe up, "What year was this?" But that was one of the reasons I insisted on working with him in person: to press for details.

Each day after we finished, I would log the outline of the story into the memory of my computer. Later, I would print it and think about the story. What was in it? What wasn't—and needed to be? Then I would start writing. If for Jake the fun was in the telling, for me the fun was in the writing. So we both got to do what made us happy.

When I was satisfied with the first draft of each story, I gave the copy to him, then rewrote it with his suggestions or changes. Often, he complained that I "stretched everything out." His oral anecdotes cut right to the chase, but I was aware that these stories would be read by people who might not know Jake Pickle, the Tenth Congressional District, or Texas politics, so I added background and detail. And always—after each draft—to his annoyance, I had more questions. Almost every night for six months I called "to check a few things" and, with unfailing poor timing, interrupted his dinner.

It was a productive system and, despite differences of opinion about what was, and wasn't, important, we were a good team. He has such wonderful stories! And because I had heard many of the stories all my life, sometimes I remembered things he had forgotten, or could see corollaries between events or people.

As we worked, the book evolved into something different from what either of us had visualized.

Jake prefers political stories with a punch line. I wanted a mix of political stories, family stories, and stories that took a larger view. We compromised on this, too. We agreed wholeheartedly on such classics as "Steamboats up the Colorado," "Bless Their Hearts," and "Bob Keckler's Cow." Other political stories, like "Ticket, Please," and "Love, Bess," have to our knowledge never been written before.

At my insistence, one of the first stories we did was "Uncle Gus and Uncle Arthur." Although both men died long before I was born, he quoted them often when I was little. Because his memories of his uncles were diverse, rather than a single incident, when I suggested a chapter about them he was surprised, saying, "But there's no story." Meaning no punch line. However, I believe Jake's memories of Gus and Arthur reveal a strong sense of family and an early respect for politics.

I talked him into doing stories about growing up in West Texas, living at Little Campus Dormitory during the Depression, and the founding of Austin radio station KVET. Some chapters, like "The White Shark" and "Dan's Debut," we did just for fun. Other chapters, like "Good-bye to LBJ and Big John," "The Civil Rights Act," and "The Navy Years," we included for their historical significance. Chapters like "The 88th Club" and "Confessions of a Rattlesnake Chili Champ" are an insider's view of Congress.

My father wanted to include three legislative chapters because the issues they addressed—Social Security, tax-exempt corporations, and pension funds—were major accomplishments of his service on the Ways and Means, Social Security, and Oversight Committees. We agonized over these three legislative chapters more than other chapters in the book because the issues are so complex, and because more work lies ahead of Congress.

As the book took shape, my father and I laughed, got teary, and fought over what—and what not—to include. Always there loomed the larger-than-life specter of Lyndon Johnson. We uncovered unexpected memories. At times, what we discovered surprised even ourselves. As we wrote about World War II and KVET, we were aided by scrapbooks my mother kept from 1939 until her death in 1952, which resurfaced after forty years when Jake and Beryl sold their Washington apartment. A bundle of antique postcards saved and given to Jake by "Handsome Harry's" son-in-law brought back the 1940s, when up-and-coming Austin men hung out at the Driskill Hotel's barbershop.

Like most great raconteurs, Jake says, "Never let the facts get in the way of a good story." Whenever the facts needed corroboration, I went to Beryl, Aunt Judith, or Uncle Joe. *They* had it straight!

I had a lot of fun writing the book. He likes being an author, too—as long as it doesn't prevent him from telling his stories in person.

Halfway through writing this book, we were in his office discussing copy with Joanna Hitchcock, Theresa May, and Dave Cohen from U.T. Press. We'd just reread the "Little Campus" chapter, when Jake repeated a prank he'd inflicted on a Little Campus dorm mate *sixty-three years ago*. As he talked, he began laughing so hard he became red in the face. Watching him doubled over with glee was contagious; Theresa, Joanna,

Dave, and I started laughing, too. I thought to myself, "It's as though it happened yesterday!" After all these years, he enjoys a good story as much as he did the first time.

And he makes us enjoy it, too. One of his great gifts is his enormous appetite for life.

This book is not a biography, documented research, or an official record of Jake Pickle's Congressional career. It's stories about his experiences in Texas, the South Pacific, and Washington, D.C., and a few of the people he's known along the way.

The stories we've written do not include every friend or person who contributed to his career—and they are legion. Out of a lifetime of stories and friends, we could not include them all. We apologize for misspellings or other inaccuracies which may occur due to the informal nature of these stories, written from memory, from a distance of more than seven decades.

As you read *Jake*, don't think of it as a book. Think of it as a *collection*!

P.P.

PART ONE

BEGINNINGS

James Jarrell Pickle, age eighteen months,
Roscoe, Texas.

West Texas
Roots

In West Texas, where I was born, the landscape is simplified, reduced to sky, mesquite and chinaberry trees, cactus, and sand. But where some people scan the horizon and see only nothingness, I saw possibilities. The days of my childhood were long and full of light. Every direction of that wide, austere landscape interested me.

Growing up in West Texas, I was a mischievous boy, steadied by family and accepted by community. My parents poured their energies into their five children. Our lives revolved around work, school, church, and each other. Whatever I am and whatever I've accomplished is a result of the discipline and laughter that were my inheritance.

My father, Joseph Binford Pickle, was born in Weakley County, Tennessee, in 1876. Pop's father, James Calvin Pickle—"Pappy"—fought with the Union Army in the Civil War. Back then, you could serve awhile; when you'd had enough or proved you were needed at home, you hitched up your mule or left on foot. After Pappy had had enough, he did just that.

Pop's mother, Louisa Dickson Pickle—"Mammy"—was tall and raw-boned. Mammy's father was half Cherokee, and *he* fought for the Confederacy. When the war was over, he refused to pledge allegiance to the United States and was imprisoned in Union City for several months, until the authorities gave up and released him.

I don't know how Pappy and Mammy resolved their families' political differences, but their union must have added some willful genes to the bloodline.

My mother, Mary Theresa Duke, was born in 1884 in Lampasas County, Texas. Mom's parents were Columbus Welcome Duke and Susan Eliza Meek. Family legend is that Mom, whose mother was a Crockett, was related to Davy Crockett. Once I bragged as much on the floor of the House of Representatives. But when it was time to put up, I had to shut up, because I couldn't prove a thing.

Pop, who was the oldest of eight children, emigrated to Texas from Fulton, Tennessee, around 1899. Back in Tennessee, two sisters had died of tuberculosis—they called it "consumption" then—and the doctor told Pop to find a dry climate. He found West Texas, which is about as dry as you can get.

He and Mom met while they were teaching in Miles, Texas, near Ballinger, in a one-room schoolhouse. They started going together, but then Mom and her folks moved to a farm in the Panhandle. That was too far apart for the sweethearts. In 1903, Pop followed her; they got married and returned to Miles.

My parents married without money and never amassed much throughout sixty years of marriage and five children, but theirs was as good a union as I ever saw. Over the years, Pop tried every way he knew to make a living. If one thing didn't work out, he threw himself into another. In the early years of their marriage, he and Mom taught school, and whenever he could, Pop picked up side jobs to bring in extra money. At the turn of the century, being a West Texas schoolteacher didn't pay much, and the family was growing. My sister Janice was born in 1904 in Miles.

Around 1910, when Mom and Pop were teaching school in Winters, Pop decided to raise a few sheep. The raising went all right, but then he had to drive the sheep to market. When the sheep came to a bridge, they spooked and refused to cross. Finally Pop had to get down on his hands and knees and lead them across the bridge. He had to do the same thing to get them under a fence. When he got home, Pop told Mom that sheep were so timid and stupid, he would never have anything to do with them again.

Then he heard that the Texas & Pacific and the Santa Fe railroads, expanding west, planned to converge in Roscoe. Roscoe was the next boom town! Mom and Pop packed up and moved to Roscoe. Pop had a new career in mind.

Pop was naturally curious, a fast reader, and a good writer. With those qualifications, but without previous experience, he started the *Roscoe Times*. A fellow named Whitten helped him set up a Linotype machine. The day Pop and Mr. Whitten were moving the Linotype into the newspaper office, a lady passing by saw them struggling, and asked what they were doing. When Pop told her, "I'm starting a news-paper—the *Roscoe Times*," she said, "Humph! I lost two bits on the last one!" Roscoe's other newspaper had folded not long before, and she was still sore about losing her subscription.

That was an omen of sorts, but Pop forged ahead. He and Mom made a good life in Roscoe. They had a pretty little house where morn-ing glories twined around the front porch. Pop was elected Roscoe's first mayor in 1907. In 1908, Jeanette was born, followed by Joe in 1910. I was born in Roscoe in 1913.

People ask why all five Pickle siblings' names start with the letter J. Janice and Jeanette were coincidence; by the time Joe came along, Mom and Pop had decided to make it a tradition—especially since Pop was a Joe, too. I was christened James Jarrell: James for my paternal grandfa-ther and Jarrell after Roscoe neighbors and friends.

But after I was about age four, everybody called me Jake. That was because for entertainment at night our family read aloud, and acted out stories and plays; in one story my character was a rascal named Jake. I was a natural Jake, and the name stuck, except with my parents. Mom and Pop always called me Jarrell.

Sure enough, Roscoe didn't become the railroad hub Pop expected, so he moved the family to Snyder. He bought a share in a newspaper run by two brothers. But after awhile, Pop realized that he was doing all the work and the brothers were doing very little. Then in 1916 he heard that Seminole was going to be an oil boom town. He wanted to get there early, so he moved the family to Seminole. Years later, he always said with a laugh, "I got there early, all right—forty years too early!"

Automobiles were starting to appear in West Texas, although they weren't as common as horses and buggies. Pop didn't know anything about cars but, as usual, he wanted to get in on the trend early, so he opened a garage in Seminole.

My three earliest memories are of Seminole, and two have to do with my disobedience. The first happened after I watched Pop lather up his beard with a straight razor. I tried to do the same thing. Mom caught me wielding the razor over a bleeding cheek and gave me a paddling.

Second, at about age four, I climbed the windmill in back of our house. Back then, there was no municipal water supply; the only way you got water was when the wind blew hard enough to turn the wheel and pump it. A wood ladder at the base of the windmill led to a platform twenty or thirty feet above the ground. One day I climbed to the top, but then I got scared and started to wail. Janice heard me and went for Mom. When Mom saw me, she was frantic. I was holding on to the platform with one hand and wiping my nose with the other. Mom started up the ladder, sweet-talking, telling me to hold on, telling me I was her precious baby—"Hold on, Jarrell, just a minute more, Mama's coming."

When she got to the top, she flung her long skirt over one arm, plucked me off the platform and carried me back down, still telling me how she loved me, "Hold on to Mother, sweetheart," she kept saying. But when we got to the ground, all hell broke loose! She paddled me *but good!* All the way down I thought I was Mama's precious darling; at the bottom, I learned that love has many faces.

Poor Mom. She was always bailing me out of scrapes or having to switch me. Pop was too soft-hearted; Mom got stuck being the disciplinarian in the family. Sometimes she'd break a switch off a cottonwood tree. I knew what *that* meant. Janice tells how once, as I watched Mom pulling off cottonwood leaves to make a switch more pliable, I stuttered, "Thaaaa's all riiiiight. You can jus' leave tho-thoooose leaves on th-there!"

My third memory of Seminole is of November 11, 1918: Armistice Day—a month after my fifth birthday. I was sitting on our back fence when I heard horns, people yelling, and loud explosions. Later, brother Joe explained they were "shooting anvils" downtown. The blacksmith would fill the crevice in his forge with gunpowder, position his heavy anvil on top, and light the powder. The anvil would fly into the air with a loud boom and come down several feet away. In Seminole, nobody had fireworks, so we shot anvils. I never experienced that again, but it made a strong impression on me.

Sure enough, the expected Seminole oil boom never materialized, so after awhile, Pop took Mom and us kids to live with Mom's parents in Lamesa.

About this time, Pop was given a team of mules and a wagon as payment of a debt. However, he had to bring them from Post, Texas, back to Lamesa, a distance of about fifty miles. Without warning, a Blue Norther hit, covering the ground with sleet and ice. The mules wouldn't move; they huddled to stay warm. Pop couldn't see any landmarks. In the dark, he found a tree and tried to climb it to get his bearings, but the trunk was too slippery. He kept trying to climb the tree anyway, just to keep warm. He was so tired all he wanted to do was lie down and sleep, but he knew if he did, he'd freeze to death. Every time he had the urge to rest, he thought "about Mary and those kids at home," and forced himself to stay on his feet. He unhitched the mules from the wagon and wrapped their reins around his hands so he wouldn't lose them in the dark. All night long he and the mules wandered the icy prairie.

Finally, the next morning he spied some telegraph lines and followed them until he came to a house, which turned out to be the John B. Slaughter Ranch. At first, when Pop burst in the door, disheveled, wild-eyed, and dirty, the cowboys thought he was a bandit. But then they realized he was half-frozen and lost, and gave him a shot of whiskey and revived him, so he was saved, and the mules, too. But by this time Pop had decided that his interests did *not* lie in ranching, especially with sheep or mules.

Throughout his life in West Texas, Pop was convinced that there was money to be made in oil and gas. He didn't expect to get rich quick—he expected to work hard, and *then* get rich! At various times he bought shares in oil and gas leases in West Texas, but they always turned out to be dry holes. He decided the thing to do was go to Burkburnett, north of Wichita Falls, where there *was* oil, and plenty of it.

In Burkburnett, he tried buying oil leases, but he couldn't scrape together much capital, and he was too honest to hustle people. From Burkburnett, he wrote Mom flowery letters, telling her how he loved her and wanted to provide for his family.

Finally, Pop had to come back to Lamesa without oil money—big or otherwise. Sister Judith was born in Lamesa in 1919. When Judith was just a few weeks old, I tried to trade her for a pig. A neighbor came to see the baby. I knew the man had a fat pig, so I tried to cut a deal whereby the man got the baby, and I got the pig. Humoring me, the man smiled and said, "Why, young fellow, that sounds like a mighty fine trade to me." Then when he got up to leave—without Judith—I ran after him and said, "Mister, you forgot your baby!"

Pop's next business venture was to go to Big Spring, where he opened a fruit stand near the railroad station. The fruit stand proved Pop's salvation. It prospered so much that he pooled resources with another man, Vic Flewellen, and opened the P&F Grocery on Main Street. But soon, Mr. Flewellen decided to go into the cotton business. Pop wasn't discouraged; he'd finally found a growing concern, and he had the people skills and gumption for retailing. So he opened the White House Grocery—named for its long white building, not because of politics—at 1901 Scurry Street.

Once the grocery business got established, he moved Mom and us kids to Big Spring. I was seven when we arrived, so Big Spring is where I grew up. Our first house was on Donley Street; then we moved to Benton Street, and then to 402 Runnels. By the time I was in high school, Pop was making enough to build a fine yellow brick house at 1800 Main. It cost $10,500, which seemed like a fortune in 1930.

Mom and Pop's prosperity was short-lived. A few years later, when the Depression really set in, they lost most of their money. Business at the White House Grocery dropped off; other customers couldn't afford to pay. A lot of people bought on credit, and Pop couldn't turn them away. In those days, rural grocers extended credit a year in advance— "till the crop's in." Each family might owe $700 or $800 by the end of the year, and the debts added up. During the worst of the Depression, Pop was carrying $25,000 in notes.

Although I know now that my parents struggled for every loaf of bread they put on the table, growing up in Big Spring was for me a halcyon experience. Joe and I had a mongrel dog, Rex, who, when he wasn't tied, would follow us to church on Sunday, walk down the aisle, and bark when he got to our pew. Pop was Southern Baptist and Mom was Methodist, but they had compromised: Mom took Janice, Jeanette, and Judith to the Methodist Church; Pop took Joe and me to First Baptist. Joe and I played sandlot baseball and were Boy Scouts and Eagle Scouts. Mom and the girls made homemade ice cream, and we kids fought over the dash. In that small town, everybody knew everybody else, and nobody locked the doors.

Once when Mom was in Lamesa visiting her folks, Pop took Joe and me to the Busy Bee Café. I was eight, and it was the first time I had eaten in a restaurant. I scanned the bill of fare, and then mortified Joe when I solemnly told the waiter, "I'll have the potted ham." Small cans of potted ham were on the shelves at the White House Grocery. It was the only thing I recognized on the menu.

Then the waiter brought out a plate of what Joe and I thought were vanilla cupcakes. We ate our food, keeping an eye on that delicious dessert—until at the end of the meal, the waiter removed the plate! They were cornbread muffins! At home, cornbread came in a skillet.

We boys didn't get out much.

The only time I ever saw my Tennessee-born father lose his temper was when a neighbor cut down one of Pop's trees. Pop thought destroying a tree in West Texas was just about a hanging offense. Sometimes he'd scan the flat horizon—that same horizon that filled me with boyish excitement—and say, "By jingo, what a Godforsaken country!" I hope there are trees in Heaven, because Pop missed them every day.

I'm told I didn't talk much until the age of three. But, as Janice says, "Once he started, it seems like he just never shut up." At Big Spring High School I was voted senior class favorite, and it had to be due to personality rather than looks, because I was the skinniest kid in town.

My senior year I was supposed to recite a speech I had written about public service at a school assembly. Halfway through the speech, every word flew right out of my head. At the time, Eugene O'Neill's play *Strange Interlude* was the rage; Groucho Marx even spoofed the title in one of his movies. So when I went blank at the assembly, I did the first thing I could think of, which was to press my fingers to my temples and say loudly to the audience, "Pardon me while I have a *strange interlude!*" The resultant laughter taught me the value of a quick recovery—and the sweet thrill of applause.

Despite being a natural ham, I never thought about being a politician. Mom and Pop thought I was so argumentative, I would make a good lawyer, so when I graduated from Big Spring High in 1932, they encouraged me in that direction. As a family, we had always talked politics around the dinner table. Pop was a populist, yellow-dog Democrat. In the early 1930s, he was elected mayor of Big Spring, supervising the construction of City Hall and the dedication of Big Spring City Park. He also had the honor of welcoming First Lady Eleanor Roosevelt to Big Spring when her plane landed to refuel.

Now, brother Joe—*he* always knew what he wanted to do! He wanted to be a newspaper man. As a child, he published *The Pickle Picayune*, filled with neighborhood happenings. As soon as he graduated from Baylor, Joe made a beeline back to Big Spring to work as a reporter for the *Big Spring Daily Herald* (now the *Big Spring Herald*). Later, he became editor, a position he held for thirty-five years, retiring after forty-three years at the paper. Janice became a librarian, and Jeanette and Judith became teachers. At the University of Texas, I was on my way to being a lawyer when I got sidetracked by politics.

I don't know how my parents, who started married life as teachers in a one-room prairie schoolhouse, managed to feed and clothe a family of seven and see all five of their children receive college degrees during the Depression. I think they were attracted to each other because each believed in education: for themselves, for others, and for their children.

Besides laughter and unconditional love, one of my parents' great gifts to me was their appreciation of hard work.

Once when I was a kid, Pop was irritated about something I had done—or hadn't done—and he told Mom, "Mary, I think I'd rather see Jarrell dead than lazy!" Startled, Mom said, "Hush, Joe. You know you don't mean that!" And Pop said heatedly, "Yes I do, because when you're dead, you don't suffer. But if you're lazy, there's no hope!"

There was plenty of hope in our house. At the age of eighty-two, I have it still.

Two

Uncle Gus and Uncle Arthur

Growing up in West Texas, I had two paternal uncles, Uncle Arthur and Uncle Gus. They were great characters.

By the mid-1920s, the White House Grocery in Big Spring had developed into a thriving business. Every member of our family worked in the store. Mom and Pop worked at the front counter, my brother Joe and I worked in the back storeroom loading sacks and candling eggs after school, and sisters Janice and Jeanette waited on customers. Baby Judith snuck goodies from the candy counter.

The oldest child in a large family, Pop was a born boss. As a little boy in Tennessee, he had cried until his parents let him go to school. The schoolhouse was a log cabin, where the children sat on benches made of split logs with peg legs. His entire life, Pop was happiest when he was learning and working. As an adult, he swung out of bed and literally hit the ground at a trot every morning, and didn't stop until he and Mom fell into bed at night.

Twenty years after leaving Tennessee, Pop heard that times back in Fulton were hard, so he wrote and offered two of his brothers jobs. So my uncles Arthur and Gus Pickle came to Big Spring to work at the White House Grocery. Uncle Arthur was a clerk and Uncle Gus ran the meat market.

*"Jarrellyou*RASCAL*you!"*
at age thirteen.

Each uncle was unique. They gave us worldly, irreverent ways of looking at things that our hard-working Baptist father could not.

Uncle Gus was tall and skinny, with a big nose and an Adam's apple the size of a hatchet. He had the most gnarled knuckles I ever saw. Whenever Joe and I got out of line, Uncle Gus would crook his finger into a knuckle and crack us on the head. Now *that* would get your attention! We called that treatment "the Uncle Gus," a name for swift punishment which endures in my family today.

Using only a heavy butcher knife and no special equipment, Uncle Gus cut meat so precisely that each steak would be exactly the same thickness at the top as at the bottom. You could have measured his steaks in micrometers, and they would have been identical. I never knew how Gus did that, and I still don't. I do know he sharpened his knives relentlessly and called them "the best in the West."

In those days before ready-sliced loaves, Gus was in charge of slicing bread at the White House Grocery. Once when Judith asked if he could slice bread thin enough for a sandwich Gus said, "Thin? I can slice it so thin you can read the Lord's Prayer through it!"

Moreover, Gus could stick his finger in a Coke bottle and pop it like a rifle. And when things in the store got slow, he would hoist his apron and kick his leg sideways, passing wind on cue, to indicate he was ready for AC-tion! These were impressive talents to a ten-year-old boy.

Uncle Arthur could not have been more physically different from Uncle Gus. Arthur was fat, with a great round stomach. He loved to tell stories about Fulton, Tennessee, and when he told a funny one, his belly rolled and pitched like a ship at sea, and his laugh came out "He-he-he!" as though squeezed from a concertina.

When a hugely pregnant woman came in the store, after she left Uncle Arthur would slip me a tow sack and say with a deadpan expression, "Follow that woman closely." Neither Uncle Arthur nor Uncle Gus would crack jokes like that when Pop or the females in the family were around, but in Joe and me Arthur and Gus had a gleefully appreciative audience, and they knew it.

In the evenings, our family would go over to Uncle Arthur and Aunt Maude's home, sit on the front porch, and listen to Uncle Arthur tell stories. His favorite stories were about Fulton and a distant relative named William Boyd Newton.

One story was about when William Boyd Newton was a newly ordained Baptist preacher, and the deacon assembled the congregation to hear church assignments. As the deacon read off the names of towns to which each new minister had been assigned, the congregation expressed its approval. The first minister came forward and the deacon announced "Fulton!" The congregation cried out, "Praise the Lord!" The next new minister was assigned to Union City, and the congregation chorused, "Hallelujah!" And so forth down the list. When the deacon got to William Boyd Newton, he read, "Mt. Moriah"—a notoriously insignificant and dismal crook in the road—and involuntarily William Boyd Newton cried out, "God-*damn*!"

Some evenings Uncle Arthur would tell about the time William Boyd Newton had been eating too many green vegetables, particularly English peas. His wife, Effie, said he ought not to eat so much roughage. But William ignored her, and sure enough, he developed terrible stomach pains. The doctor was summoned. The physician prescribed Ipecac, and after Effie gave her husband a stout dose, they sat down at the table and waited. It wasn't long before William began to vomit up his excess. Small green peas bounced ominously across the table. Determined to have the last word, William Boyd Newton straightened up and said, "Effie, I *told* you those damn peas weren't done!"

Arthur told stories like these over and over again, and we laughed at them just as hard every time. Today, when I repeat my own stories, I remember Aunt Maude's great patience in listening to Uncle Arthur. My family does the same thing with me.

I was the mischievous kid in our family. Although I had been christened James Jarrell, it was a family joke that Pop hardly ever called me Jarrell. Frequently, he was either remembering my last—or discovering my newest—shenanigan, and when he saw me he'd automatically say, "Jarrellyourascalyou!"

Whenever Joe or I pulled some prank or did something stupid, Uncle Arthur would look at us, shake his head ruefully, and say, "I don't believe that boy will ever make Congress."

After I graduated from Big Spring High School, I went off to Austin and the University of Texas, and in a sense I never came home again. When I got involved in campus politics, there was a small item in the *Big Spring Daily Herald* that I had been elected President of the U.T. Student Body. The next time I was in Big Spring I went to visit Uncle Arthur, whose health was failing. Arthur's only comment about my political "career" was predictably dry. He said, "Well, Jarrell, I see you're doing all right at State."

And I nodded and said, "Uncle Arthur, tell me again about William Boyd Newton."

Uncle Arthur and Uncle Gus, I *did* make Congress—and I took a lot of you with me.

*Little Campus Dormitory in the 1920s,
about a decade before Jake arrived at the
University of Texas.*

Little
Campus

I enrolled as a freshman at the University of Texas in the fall of 1932, driven from Big Spring to Austin by my father in his open-air Oldsmobile. The engine overheated several times, so the trip took twelve hours. We brought along two other Big Spring boys, Clyde and George Thomas. Because it was the Depression, my father charged their parents a few dollars so he could buy gas for the long drive to and from West Texas.

We checked into the Little Campus Dormitory, a complex of dun-colored brick, limestone, and frame buildings on the outskirts of the U.T. campus at 19th Street (now Martin Luther King Boulevard) and East Avenue (today Interstate Highway 35). During the Depression, Little Campus, built in 1858 as the Texas Asylum for the Blind, was known as "the poor boys' dorm."

Little Campus had been recommended by Big Spring boys Howard Smith and Walton Morrison, who were three years ahead of me. My first Little Campus roommate was Lon Ogg from Houston. Later, when we were allowed to pick our own roommates, I roomed with my life-long friend from Big Spring, T. J. "Toddy" Williamson.

In the thirties the Little Campus compound rambled all over the hill overlooking East Avenue, and consisted of an administration building and five dorms—buildings A–E. Today, only two Little Campus structures remain. One, the administration building–resident manager's home, was saved from demolition because General George Armstrong Custer had lived there during the winter of 1865–1866, so it was thought to have historical significance. To me, Little Campus' historical significance postdates—and supersedes—General Custer. It was where my life in politics and my love affair with the University of Texas and Austin began.

Before my father left to drive back to Big Spring, he gave me sixty-five dollars. Twenty-five dollars paid for a room at Little Campus the first semester; another twenty-five paid my tuition. The other fifteen dollars was for books, supplies—and food!

So I had to get a job, fast—and I did, taking over a Little Campus milk route vacated by a graduating senior. In this arrangement I placed a phone order every day with a dairy farmer near Manor. The next day, the farmer would deliver the milk before 6 A.M. just inside the fence between dormitories A and B on East Avenue. By leaving my window cracked, I could hear the clink of bottles. I would jump out of bed, throw on clothes, and stumble downstairs. Then I would trudge up and down the stairs of each dorm, leaving the ordered pints and quarts outside the doors to the rooms.

A continual problem was my dormmates' sport of "bowling with bottles," spinning empties down Little Campus' long halls. Broken bottles came out of my profit. It was said around Little Campus that Pickle could hear the sound of glass rolling anywhere in the complex, and would materialize from thin air to grab it before impact. When a bottle *did* break, I confess I scoured the doorsteps of neighborhood houses for replacements. At night I left the empties beside the East Avenue fence, so the whole routine could begin again the next morning.

Every day I handled thirty or forty orders for milk. I cleared about a penny a bottle, which, over a month's time, earned me twenty-five or thirty dollars. With that money I could afford to buy one good meal a day, aside from breakfast, which Toddy and I ate in our room.

In those days, milk, cereal, and hard rolls were our mainstays. The milk was on me! Almost everybody kept a stash of food in a wooden box, which we hoisted by pulley to the ceiling of our room, and secured by tying the rope to a radiator. We oiled the rope to discourage ants and cockroaches. Every morning we would get our milk, lower the box, pour milk into bowls, take out a couple of rolls, and eat breakfast. Afterward, we would wash our bowls in the sink, put everything back in the box and hoist it up to the ceiling.

Later, I got a laundry route. I gathered the boys' shirts and pants and took them to Nick Lenz Cleaners on Congress Avenue. About all I got out of that deal was clean shirts, plus a little pocket change. But it supplied my laundry.

Between delivering milk and picking up laundry, I got acquainted with every resident of Little Campus. I knew all their hometowns, how many brothers and sisters they had, what they were studying. It was my first experience at networking, although I didn't know it at the time.

My sophomore year, Harvey "Butch" Voelker and I got part-time jobs at the Engineering Building for twenty-five cents an hour. T. U. Taylor, the school's legendary dean, had laid out a turnip patch on the southeast side of the Engineering Building. Often, as Butch and I were carrying out the building's trash bins, one of us would "stumble," bend over to retrieve the trash, and quick pull up a few turnips. Out of sight in our locked janitor's closet on the third floor, we would wash and slice them and eat them raw. We country boys thought those turnips tasted as luscious as watermelon. I found out years later that Dean Taylor, whose office in the Engineering Building had a bird's-eye view of the turnip patch, enjoyed standing at his window watching our act. Sometimes, he would even call other professors to look, chortling, "Watch this. There! Did you see them do that?" Maybe he planted those turnips just to watch us perform. But we never knew he was wise to us, and he never begrudged us his turnips.

My junior year I was hired as a Texas Senate page by Senator Arthur Duggan from Littlefield. That job paid the princely sum of seventy-five dollars a month! For awhile I was so flush that on the way home from the Capitol every morning, I would stop at Cuneo's Bakery and buy sweet pecan rolls for most of the second floor of my dorm. In the depths of the Depression, pecan rolls and hot chocolate were like elixir from Heaven. All my friends were happy about *that* job.

When the legislative session ended, I secured a job as night watchman at the Capitol. We had to punch a watchman's clock every hour on the hour. Floyd Inks, who was Capitol night supervisor, suspected I caught a few winks between punch-ins. When he made his rounds, he always cleared his throat or whistled as he came down the hall.

At 10 P.M., we closed the doors to the Capitol. From then on, through the long hours of the morning, we had time to kill. The Capitol had just gotten a brand new terrazzo floor, and its surface was smooth and inviting. I sometimes rode a borrowed bicycle to work, and late at night we watchmen would jump on that bike and ride like the wind from one end of the west wing to the east wing, a distance of three blocks. I'm one of the few human beings who know what it's like to zoom through the Capitol Rotunda at forty miles an hour—no friction or bumps! But we forgot about skid marks, and when they were discovered, I was fired. Senator G. H. Nelson from Lubbock appealed on my behalf and got me reinstated.

But my best job was waiting tables at Mrs. Martha Jacobsen's boarding house at 1613 Sabine Street. Mrs. Jacobsen had a couple of boarders and fed another thirty boys with meal tickets. If she had a soft spot for you, she'd give you a job, but because so many boys wanted jobs, we only worked part time.

Mrs. Jacobsen saved my life. She was my mother away from home. She took a liking to me. I always knew that no matter how hard things got, I could count on one good meal a day at Mrs. Jacobsen's. Often on Sunday, she would phone me at Little Campus and say in her German accent, "Mr. Pickle, I'm a little short-handed. Can you help me out?" Of course, I knew that Mrs. Jacobsen had hungry boys standing in line; she was helping *me* out. But I would run down there as fast as I could. Bustling around the kitchen, she'd say good-naturedly, "Was ist los? Alles was nicht fest gebunden ist!" ("What's the matter? Everything's OK if nothing's wrong!")

At Mrs. Jacobsen's, I cleared tables and scraped dishes. Butch Voelker and I worked a lot of shifts together. He washed and I dried. Thirty boys create a lot of dirty dishes, but Butch and I thought we were the best and fastest dishwashers in Austin. In return for working, we got that meal free. The next meal—the one we didn't work—we had to pay.

Like the rest of us, Mrs. Jacobsen, who was a widow, scrounged to make a living. I don't know how she fed so many of us. We ate a lot of okra, beef stew, chicken and dumplings, black-eyed peas, peach cobbler, banana pudding—and an ocean of red pinto beans. Mrs. Jacobsen was the hardest-working, most determined woman I ever knew, and one of the kindest. God bless her soul.

So I was enrolled in the university, I had a room—and I ate two meals a day (plus an occasional turnip). I was fixed!

When I first arrived in Austin, I thought about Big Spring and my folks a lot, but so many other Big Spring boys—like John Stripling, Vestal Michael and his brother, Jimmy Jones, and Beverly Rockhold— were living at Little Campus that I didn't get too homesick. We pitched horseshoes and took sunbaths in the courtyards between dorms. Street-cars ran right by the dorm; we could ride all the way to the Deep Eddy swimming pool for ten cents. We played pass 'n' touch football where IH 35 is today. We had our own handball court and gym, and once, wearing rubber rain slickers, we had a spectacular rotten egg fight in the gym. We couldn't afford to join a fraternity, so we were our own fraternity. Austin's population was less than 50,000 in the early thirties, but it was the big time to me. The university had about 4,000 students. The population of Little Campus, so-called because we were part of, yet geographically separate from the rest of the campus, was about 130 students.

I joined the university swim team and also the wrestling team. I was so wiry and skinny that when I wrestled, I had to best my opponents with cunning instead of brawn. When I got lucky and won a few matches, I went around bragging that I had a "devastating scissors hold." A few of the boys in the dorm got tired of listening to me, and decided to enter me in a wrestling contest. They talked a reporter for the *Daily Texan* into running a story about my wrestling accomplishments, and how I was going to represent Little Campus in an upcoming competi-tion. One morning I was appalled to read in the *Texan* that I would take on all comers in my weight class (about 145 pounds) in the upcoming Fight Night at Gregory Gym.

However, I also knew that if I didn't accept the challenge, I would be kidded unmercifully in the dorm from then on. The only thing I could do was figure out a way to survive Fight Night. So I got T. O. Dillard, a friend and winning member of the wrestling team, to show me a few of his favorite holds, especially how to pin an opponent's shoulders to the mat. T. O. taught me some moves, but in the process, he worked me over good! When I woke up the morning of Fight Night, I hurt so bad I was half sick. It was an effort to walk upright.

During my first match, when my opponent grabbed me, the pain and shock went through my system like electricity! It hurt so much, I furiously wrapped my legs around his neck and got him in a scissors hold. In short order, he patted the mat, signifying surrender.

The second match went much the same; my opponent hurt me so much that I flew into a rage, attacked, and subdued him. But by the third match, I was getting tired. My opponent was well-built, genial Ed Stebbins. I knew I was too tired to overpower Ed; my only hope was to get an early advantage. So as soon as the referee's whistle blew, signaling the beginning of the match, I jumped on old Ed and held on for dear life. And that's how I won—I stayed on top and kept him pinned to the mat. It was a dull match, but eventually I was declared the winner!

You can imagine my pleasure when I returned to Little Campus with my bronze wrestling medal. I went up and down the halls, wanting to crow about my glorious victories and my "devastating scissors hold," but all I saw of my dormmates were the backs of their heads as they ducked around the corner.

We boys adopted a stray dog, a little mixed breed we named Elsie D—after L(ittle) C(ampus) Dorm. Many of us had left dogs behind at home, so Elsie was everybody's mascot. We fed Elsie scraps brought back to our rooms. Elsie had the run of the place, and ranged far and wide. Eventually, of course, she got pregnant. When Elsie was about to deliver puppies, word spread and boys rushed back to the dorm. Toddy and I took Elsie to our room, where she crawled under Toddy's bed. Many of us witnessed Elsie giving birth, the most basic sex education some of us had ever received. We all felt like proud papas. Our Elsie was one of a long line of Little Campus Elsie D's. Today I have a concrete marker, given to me by a later Little Campus resident, that marked the grave of an Elsie from 1946.

Little Campus rooms were spartan. Each room had two narrow iron beds with mattresses, a sink, and a small wooden desk and chair. Each floor shared a gang lavatory with showers and toilets. On the first floor of each dorm, a telephone hung on one wall. When it rang, if you were lucky somebody walking by answered the phone and hollered for you. But we didn't get many calls, especially long distance. Contact with the folks back home was usually by mail.

Mail was delivered to the Little Campus administration building and sorted into wooden pigeonholes. The first thing we looked for when we got out of class was a letter from home. Mothers sent cookies and candy now and then; mine did, anyway. My folks put five kids through college, so instead of money, they sent sweets. When any of us got a package from home, the other boys guessed—hoped—it was something to eat. Somehow, Perry Pickett from Fort Worth always knew when I got a package. He would show up in my room, look up at the wooden box hanging from the ceiling and crow, "Why, Pickle, I do believe I smell cookies." One time I decided to set a trap for Pickett— literally. He lowered the box, laughing and congratulating me on my mother's fine cooking. But when he reached up inside, a mousetrap went off, snapping his fingers. He let go of the rope and the heavy wooden box came crashing down on his feet.

Perry Pickett was always talking big and walking loud. Another time Jack Flock and I decided to put Pickett in his place. One night we slipped into his room and in the dark looped a rope around his bed while he was sleeping. Then we doused him with a bucket of chemically treated water and, while he was sputtering and struggling to get free, whacked him several times with a leather Sam Browne military belt. Naturally, he was mad as hell. Flock and I ran for the door. Pickett freed himself and headed for my room. I was in bed, feigning sleep. He leaned over and listened to my breathing for a full five minutes. He ran to Flock's room and listened to him, too. The next morning, when we saw Pickett airing his wet, smelly mattress outside Building A, we asked innocently, "Pickett, did something happen last night?" He grumbled, "I'm on to you guys. I know who did it. I'm too smart for Flock and Pickle!" That became a saying around Little Campus, and has endured all these years. Even today when I talk about out-maneuvering some- one, I'll say, "Too smart for Flock and Pickle!"

A favorite practice in those days was to "stack a room." We'd turn everything in a room upside down, including the bed, and NAIL IT TO THE CEILING! Of course, you had to have an accomplice who could lift and tie knots. Stacking a room was the ultimate prank, and required delicate timing and nerves of steel. My room was stacked once by Homer Helton from Houston. It was also stacked another time, but it wasn't a professional job. It was done by amateurs; they didn't even know what to do.

Another great Little Campus character was Thurman "Culp" Krueger from Houston. He roomed with Arthur Wende in Dormitory A. Krueger was always pulling terrible pranks. Even I had a hard time keeping ahead of Krueger. One night Toddy Williamson and I decided to fix Krueger. Paul Barker, a graduate chemistry student living in Dormitory B, mixed up a bucket of chemicals. Nothing toxic, but it was oily and the fumes made you half sick. We knew Krueger's bed was closest to the door. So we fastened a rope to Krueger's doorknob and tied it to the doorknob across the hall. Then we climbed on a chair and emptied the bucket through the transom onto Krueger's head. When he tried to get us, he couldn't open the door.

My senior year, my reputation as a prankster boomeranged. Little Campus' resident manager R. V. Shirley and his wife were living in the Custer building. Little Campus residents carried on a running feud with all managers: we would claim the floors weren't clean, or the mail wasn't delivered on time, or something. Some of the students decided to hang Shirley in effigy. The next morning a life-size dummy wearing a sign—"R. V. Shirley"—dangled from the front balcony of the Custer building, in full view of 18th Street. Because I was a floor manager at the time and had a passkey, the rumor spread: "Pickle must have done it." Actually, I had nothing to do with it. Later, I found out that Dick Waite, Joe Coltharp, and J. G. Stockard were the culprits, although they never admitted it. That spring, I was removed as floor manager. It was one of the few times I *was* innocent!

These high jinks sound terrible, but everybody did them. It was how we entertained ourselves and let off steam. The loyalties, alliances, and rivalries we formed at Little Campus lasted a lifetime. Twenty-five years after we left Little Campus, one night then–State Senator Culp Krueger and I were drinking at Austin's Terrace Motor Hotel, and I admitted to him that Toddy Williamson and I "might" have been the ones who poured water through his transom. Krueger jumped out of his chair and cried, "By God, Pickle, I'll pass a Senate resolution denouncing you!" He went immediately to the phone and called his old roommate, Arthur Wende, in Houston; gleefully they vowed revenge.

Girls weren't allowed in our rooms at Little Campus, of course. In fact, girls were exotic creatures all around. I remember the first time I picked up a date at Littlefield Dorm, I was scared to death. The only nice pants I owned were those I was wearing, and my mother had patched them so many times the seat was like a quilt. I worried that my jacket would ride up in back and expose the patches. Sometimes, we boys attended "Germans"—dances at sorority and fraternity houses— or the old Millet Opera House on East 9th (today the Austin Club). But generally, a real date cost more money than Little Campus boys had.

Where girls were concerned, we had to be innovative. Once we held a fall dance in Little Campus' gymnasium. One of the buildings in the complex had an enormous second-floor room, perhaps used to drill soldiers during World War I. But it was our basketball court and gym. We couldn't afford store-bought decorations, so we used what was available. We found this old boy (he was in his thirties, which seemed old to us) who was an unemployed decorator, and he agreed to transform our brick gym into fantasy land.

A bunch of us piled into jalopies and drove toward La Grange, where somebody knew land that had the best Spanish moss. Somewhere in the creek bottoms—I couldn't find it again if I tried—we climbed live oaks and with broomsticks knocked down moss, which we piled into washtubs. Then we hauled everything back to Austin.

We strung wires across the ceiling of the gym, crisscrossing at right angles, and draped the Spanish moss from the wires. The decorator attached butcher paper to the walls, on which he painted fish, coral, sunken galleons, and deep-sea divers. Then he fashioned paper lanterns, and we hung them from the wires so that they appeared to be floating in the Spanish moss. I have no idea what paper lanterns had to do with an underwater fantasy. We were after effect, not reality.

The night of the dance, when we dimmed the lights and brought in our dates, they oohed and aahed. In fact, it looked so nice, we decided to throw *another* party the following weekend—which meant no basketball in "Davy Jones' gym" all week. A small sacrifice to dazzle the ladies.

By my sophomore year I was beginning to get invitations to social events on campus. This was due to my ability to talk rather than my ability to pay for anything. Many of these sought-after invitations required a tux. Of course, I didn't have a tux. I don't think anybody else at Little Campus had one, either. So I talked Toddy Williamson into buying a tux with me. We went to Wilcox men's store on Congress Avenue, put three dollars down and pledged to pay one dollar a month. I was six feet tall, and so skinny I only weighed 140 pounds soaking wet; Toddy was a short five feet six inches. Whenever it was Toddy's turn to wear the tux, he had to roll up the pants, tuck the sleeves, and avoid strenuous dance numbers. I wore that tux for years. Toddy wore it a few times. If there ever was a con job done on a close friend, it was me talking Toddy into sharing that tux.

Most Little Campus students took five classes a semester, and a lot of us worked. Few of us had typewriters, so we wrote papers in longhand. None of us had the money to go anywhere, or drink much, so after dinner we went back to our rooms and studied. I was a decent, but not particularly diligent, student. I guess you could say I was more active in other fields. Politics was one.

I got my first experience in politics while at Little Campus. In the early thirties, U.T. fraternities were divided between the "Little Clique" and the "Big Clique"—the People's Party. The fraternities routinely nominated and elected campus officers. In order to extend their influence, campus organizations designated one person from each dorm as their representative. Allan Walker from High Roll, New Mexico, was a senior law student and a member of Delta Theta Phi, U.T.'s non-social law fraternity. My sophomore year, I ran for Student Assembly from Little Campus; the following year I was elected chairman of the Judiciary Council. That's how I met Allan Walker.

I joined Delta Theta Phi as a pre-law student my junior year, in anticipation of attending law school full time. Allan and I developed a close friendship and he got me admitted as a member of Delta Theta Phi. When Allan graduated, I became the People's Party Little Campus representative.

My job was to participate in caucuses in which we discussed potential candidates for office. Or I would introduce the People's Party candidate around Little Campus. John Connally, Joe Kilgore, and lots of other fellows were in Delta Theta Phi, and that's how I got to know them. We joked that we had so little money, Delta Theta Phi stood for "a dollar thirty-five." It was almost true.

People like us, who weren't affiliated with a social fraternity, were known as independents. After a while, the fraternity men got uneasy because we independents, called "barbs" (short for barbarians), began to influence their caucuses. So the fraternity cliques banned barb participation in their events. That was the biggest mistake they ever made, because it forced us barbs to form our own alliance, which we did. We formed an independent party and ran our own slate.

By my junior year, I was being mentioned as a candidate for student body president, but I declined to run. In those days, after two years of undergraduate courses, you could move into law school your third year and, if you did well, graduate with a law degree after five years, total. My junior year I moved into law courses, and I planned to devote my time and energies to law for the next three years. By then I knew a lot of people on campus, not just Little Campus.

Popular independent Jimmy Brinkley from Houston—called "Cousin" Brinkley because whenever he saw you on campus he'd say, "How you doin', cousin?"—ran for student body president that year, and won. So we knew it could be done.

By my fourth year, I wasn't doing too well in my law courses. They just didn't hold my attention. I had failed a few classes, and kind of lost interest in a career in law. I returned to the School of Arts and Sciences, and planned to graduate with a government degree. So I decided to run for president after all.

In the spring of 1937 I filed for U.T. student body president. I was an independent, but I had the backing of Delta Theta Phi. There were a lot more independents than fraternity members on campus; there are *always* more have-nots than haves. The question was, how could we get all the independents to support one candidate—me? That was a problem, but the solution taught me one of the most important political lessons I ever learned.

My announced opponent for president was Ramsey Moore, a member of Phi Psi fraternity. Unknown to either Moore or me, Bob Eckhardt of Austin, a popular former editor of the *Texas Ranger* humor magazine, decided *he* was going to run for president, too. My friends tried to talk him out of it, but Eckhardt, then and now a free-thinking man (and later my colleague in the U.S. House of Representatives) was adamant. So we two barbs found ourselves running against one fraternity candidate. It was obvious we would split the vote, and the frat man would win.

Luckily, some fraternities supported us. One of my good friends was Joel Westbrook, a member of the SAE fraternity. Joel was a character. His campus nickname was "Colonel Westbrook" because he was famous for concocting potent mint juleps.

Through Joel, I knew a lot of SAEs and had their support. I think it was John Connally and Joel who came up with a strategy: we would force a runoff between the top two candidates. An informal student poll conducted by classmate Joe Belden showed me running behind the fraternity candidate and ahead of Eckhardt, which meant that in a field of three, I was number two. U.T.'s student constitution already contained a provision whereby issues could be placed on the ballot as a result of student "initiative and referendum."

My supporters took petitions demanding a runoff between the top two candidates into every dorm, boarding house, and fraternity on campus until we got enough signatures to get the issue on the ballot.

And here is the valuable lesson I learned: a candidate needs an issue to arouse people. Our issue was the democratic appeal of a runoff, so that the frats would no longer control campus politics. We urged students to be fair, be democratic. To search their conscience and "do the right thing."

And not only did people sign our petition, they became inflamed! Our plea for democracy caught everybody's fancy—so much so that on election day, lo and behold, *I* was high man on the ticket! Moore was second, and Eckhardt third. We'd fought hard for a runoff we didn't need—and which might even defeat me.

Frankly, we barbs thought about ignoring the petitions or destroying them. However, I wasn't comfortable with that. I went to Dean of Students Arno Nowotny, whom I admired, and asked for his advice. We talked a long time. Finally, when Nowotny counseled me that a runoff really *was* "the right thing to do," I knew he was right. When the runoff was held, to my enormous relief, I won anyway. By this time I was living in the Delta Theta Phi house on Rio Grande Street, but I still had the support of the boys at Little Campus. Those milk and laundry routes paid off in more ways than one.

I've always been proud that John Connally served as my campaign manager in 1937. The following year, when Connally successfully ran for student body president, I managed *his* campaign. I always reminded John: me first!

The skills I learned during those campaigns helped me in the years ahead, when I was involved in dozens of campaigns on a state and national level, including my own Congressional race. But it all started at Little Campus.

I graduated from the University of Texas in 1938, after six years as an undergraduate (my unsuccessful detour into law took almost two years). In the almost sixty years since I graduated, I have often thought of the opportunities that were mine because I lived in "the poor boys' dorm" and, later, the Delta Theta Phi house. So many people helped me along the way. I was much older before I realized the generosity of spirit that took during hard times.

In those old barracks-like structures I aligned myself with young men who couldn't have attended the University of Texas if there hadn't been a Little Campus. Physically and economically we were isolated from the main campus, but united in a desire to get an education and make something of ourselves.

From Little Campus during the thirties emerged men who became leaders of their generation. Perry Pickett became a district judge in Midland. Culp Krueger became a Texas state senator. Homer Stevenson became a member of the Texas Court of Civil Appeals in Beaumont. Allan Walker became a district judge in New Mexico. Charles Bintliff, Paul Barker, Toddy Williamson, and Clyde Thomas became physicians. George Thomas, Jack Flock, Duke Taylor, Frank Knapp, and Hiram

Berry became attorneys. Vince Taylor became Assistant Attorney General of Texas. Richard Gonzalez became a vice president of Humble Oil; Arthur Wende was an executive for Humble, too. Lon Ogg and Butch Voelker became geologists. Joe Belden, who took the poll during our student body election, founded the Texas Poll, an organization which predated the Gallup Poll. Lee Allison became a rancher. Jimmy Spaulding sold mortuary supplies all over Texas. Phi Beta Kappa student Brockman Horne became Assistant National Administrator for the General Services Administration. James Voss became president of Cal-Tex Refinery. Jim McKay became a judge in San Antonio. Ralph Flannigan, Bob Tarleton, Hondo Crouch, and Adolph Keifer swam in Olympic competition, and Tex Robertson was the coach who took them there. Beleaguered Little Campus resident manager R. V. Shirley became an administrator at the U.S. Library of Congress.

The list goes on and on.

In the early 1980s, when U.T. was threatening to raze Little Campus, enough of us "poor boys" raised a fuss that some members of the Board of Regents were reluctant to force the issue; others, like Jane Weinert and Ed Clark, openly supported us. Past U.T. President Peter Flawn and former Regents Tom Law and Janey Briscoe were supporters, as well. By this time, many people appreciated fine old buildings and wanted to preserve the university's history.

One time, a date for demolition of the entire complex was actually set. Former Ambassador to Australia and Regent Ed Clark, a friend of mine, listened to the demolition plan outlined by U.T. Chancellor E. Don Walker. Clark scratched his head, then said mildly in his high, singsong East Texas drawl, "Well, Mr. Chancellor, if you move to do that, I want you to know that I purr-sonally will have a war-raant for your a-rrest and throw your ass in jail within . . . the . . . HOUR." *That* got everybody's attention!

Eventually most of the buildings at Little Campus were demolished. We couldn't save them all, but with the help of civilian-activist Susan Cox, a "little old lady in white tennis shoes," we saved two. When the buildings went down, I drove over, paid a man twenty dollars, and loaded the trunk of my car full of the dun-colored bricks scattered all over the ground. Beryl and I paved the sidewalk in back of our townhouse with those bricks. I walk on a little bit of Little Campus every day.

Over the years, we've hosted half a dozen Little Campus reunions. Culp Krueger and I organized reunions on the grounds of Little Campus, the State Capitol, and of course, Scholz Beer Garden. Jimmy Spaulding organized reunions after Krueger's death. Our reunions have attracted Little Campus "boys"—old men now—from all over the country. Always, we said we wanted to get together "one more time."

We're still getting together. We're still talking about the *next* time.

Someday, someone should write the definitive history of Little Campus. It would be a best-seller.

But that's another story!

PART TWO

ON MY OWN

Four

My First Meeting with LBJ

When Congress established the National Youth Administration in the 1930s to provide jobs for young people coming out of the Depression, I was one of the beneficiaries. After I graduated from U.T. in 1938, I was hired as an NYA area supervisor by A. W. Brisbin, the NYA District Director in Waco, and sent to Stephenville, Texas. My beginning NYA salary was a princely $100 a month. Later, NYA transferred me to Waco, and then to Palestine in East Texas.

In Stephenville and Palestine, my responsibility was to oversee local NYA projects: a girl's residence center in Stephenville, schools in Dublin and Comanche, and a sawmill outside Palestine. In Waco, I handled public relations, mostly writing NYA press releases and speeches.

In Stephenville, I had the good fortune to be introduced by my former U.T. classmate Billy Oxford, a Stephenville boy, to Mrs. Robert Carlton, a widow who took in boarders. Mrs. Carlton loved to play bridge. On occasion she had ladies in for a game; whenever somebody couldn't make it, I filled in as a fourth. My bridge was mediocre, but I never refused a game because Mrs. Carlton served cake at her bridge parties. In those days I was lean and hungry, and I mean that literally. The ladies would tease me and pass the cake around. I held the cards with one hand, shoveled in cake with the other, and tried not to talk with my mouth full.

In Waco, I shared a room with my Big Spring friend Tom Beasley, then a reporter for the *Waco News Tribune* (now the *Waco Tribune-Herald*). The room cost about three dollars a day, and we split the cost. Tom and I enjoyed being on our own and probably saw ourselves as glamorous bachelors, but we led a no-frills existence. We had no family within 250 miles, and little money. At night we could get a good meal for fifty cents, but afterward, about all we could afford to do was go back to the Milner and go to sleep.

When I was transferred to Palestine, I boarded at the home of Mrs. Edward Montgomery, another kind widow, whose sons, Ed and Pete, had been my U.T. classmates.

Both Mrs. Carlton and Mrs. Montgomery were from old, respected families. Boarding in their homes gave me recognition within the community and made me feel less like the outsider I was. During those waning days of the Depression, I felt lucky to have a job, *any job*—especially one that gave me a shot at making something of myself.

Somewhere along the way, I bought a used car, a snub-nosed black 1932 Chevy coupe, which I nicknamed "the Bullet." I spent most of my time in the Bullet, driving the counties in my NYA district.

I was in Palestine in 1940 when my friend and former classmate John Connally passed through Palestine on the train, en route to Washington, D.C., where he was administrative assistant for Congressman Lyndon Johnson. Connally called me up from the train station with an intriguing offer: how would I like to come to Austin, as NYA Area Director?

Would I? I told Connally, "Man, I'll be there tomorrow!" Connally said dryly, "Next week will be soon enough."

So in the fall of 1940, after two years of living like a nomad, I moved back to Austin with joy in my heart. My new NYA district mirrored Johnson's own Tenth Congressional District. Somehow Johnson had set that up, so that even when he was away in Washington for months on end, he could keep an eye and ear on what was happening back home.

In addition to my regular NYA supervisory duties, as I traveled about my—and Johnson's—district, I made time to drop in on every mayor, school superintendent, postmaster, and newspaper editor in town—*especially* the newspaper editors. I asked a few questions, listened a lot, and took the pulse of the community. Once a week, I sat down and wrote a lengthy report to Johnson. I told him what people were talking about, who was worried about what, and why. It was a great system, although I didn't appreciate it as much as I worried about failing to detect a mood or trend. I knew this was my big chance. I didn't want to screw it up.

All this time, I had only corresponded with Johnson, or talked with him by phone. Also, I think I shook hands with him once or twice, in a group. But we had never had a personal, one-on-one meeting.

My big break came in early 1941, when I was sent to Washington to discuss with Johnson a proposed highway to be built from Austin to Burnet, and back to Austin—a scenic loop which would parallel the Colorado River and the growing chain of Highland Lakes. I don't know how serious these plans were (and indeed that particular highway never materialized), but since the NYA and the Texas Highway Commission were under consideration to construct it, as Area Director I got a trip to Washington at government expense.

In Washington, I checked into the Dodge Hotel, about four blocks from the Capitol. When I say "checked in," I mean I was entitled to a cot in the basement. The Congressman and Lady Bird lived in an apartment in the Dodge Hotel. Johnson had worked a deal with the hotel management so that "his boys" coming in and out of Washington could stay in the basement for something like one dollar a night. A lot of early Johnson confederates stayed there at one time or another: Walter Jenkins, John Connally, Charlie Henderson, John Singleton, Warren Cunningham, Jim Langdom, myself, and I don't know how many others.

"Lyndon's boys" at the Dodge Hotel slept below ground in a long, narrow labyrinth crowded with steam pipes and boxes. We shared a common john down the hall, and hung our clothes from pipes in the ceiling. It might have been depressing, except that we were there only late at night, when we lay down on a cot and were asleep instantly. War was brewing, and Washington was an exciting place. We had meetings to attend, bars and restaurants to frequent, and pretty women to smile at. It was a heady time. We were young, poor, and ambitious. In the basement of the Dodge Hotel, we were also warm.

Not long after my arrival at the Dodge Hotel, I received the summons: L. E. "Luther" Jones and I were to meet with the Congressman at 10 o'clock Sunday morning. Years before, Luther had been one of Johnson's high school debate students; now he was on Johnson's Washington staff. I already knew and respected Luther because we had been Delta Theta Phi law fraternity brothers at U.T. As I prepared myself for the big meeting, Luther kept telling me how important LBJ was, how the Congressman was going places, and how, if I played my cards right, I could go places, too. We all could.

"You should watch him, Pickle!" Luther said. "He's amazing. He'll have you doing things you never thought possible. Big things! Important things!"

Luther went on like this long enough to get me really nervous. Then we took the elevator upstairs, to Johnson's apartment.

We knew that Lady Bird was out of town. We knocked on the door, which was ajar. At first there was no answer, then a voice—the Congressman's—called out, "C'mon in! You fellows come in here!"

We walked through the apartment, and Johnson called again. "I'm in here. Luther! Jake! Come on in!"

We turned the corner. Johnson was on the throne! He was wearing striped pajamas, or at least the tops. The bottoms were on the floor, around his feet. I ducked back behind the door, but poor Luther was being summoned by name. He stuck his head around the bathroom door and spoke to the Congressman. Occasionally, I joined in. We conversed like this for a while, Luther and I standing in the bedroom, Johnson attending to his business in the bathroom. I stood around the corner, out of sight, grinning like hell. Luther, trying to carry on a normal conversation with his boss, couldn't afford to let laughter creep into his voice. He kept his eyes on the carpet instead of me.

They went on like this for a few minutes; then Johnson called, "Luther, hand me some more paper!" And Luther did.

Finally, there was the sound of rushing water, and Johnson appeared in the bedroom in his pajamas. He unrolled a map of the proposed highway, and we discussed the road for an hour. Nothing was settled, but the meeting gave Johnson the chance to observe me, and vice versa. Of course, I had already observed more of Johnson that day than I had anticipated!

Years later, I heard of similar incidents, where Johnson conducted business from the bathroom. It was a habit that embarrassed people and threw them off balance. Some, especially the Kennedy camp, found this habit particularly disgusting, and even frightening. They believed Johnson used it to intimidate and humiliate subordinates.

That was probably true in some cases. But I knew Lyndon Johnson for thirty years, and I believe that although he was aware of the effect this habit had on people, he didn't care. I never knew Lyndon Johnson's mind to be at rest. Even in moments of solitude, like just before he slid into sleep, he was thinking, planning, and scheming. To Johnson, the bathroom, a natural spot for reflection, was where he often did his best thinking, and just one more place to plot strategy with his lieutenants.

But if I had looked forward to a personal meeting, I sure got one!

Incidentally, I told this story to Robert Caro when he was researching his first book about LBJ, *The Path to Power*, but I instructed Caro to leave my name out of the story. This is the first time I've gone on record. As I told Caro, there were lots of things about Johnson that were unsettling. You had to look beyond them, to what the man accomplished. He was always testing you. He was always testing his power.

That day in 1941, as we left Johnson's room, I couldn't resist sticking it to Luther. "You're right," I said. "Johnson *does* have you doing things you never thought possible. Important things!

"For instance, I notice you did a fine job of handing him that paper!"

Luther took it good-naturedly.

I was transferred by the NYA three more times—to Beaumont, back to Austin, then to Houston—until late 1941, when I left the NYA to join Johnson's re-election campaign. By this time, just after Pearl Harbor, Johnson and Connally had received commissions in the Navy and were headed overseas. They called from California and asked me to travel the Tenth Congressional District, gathering names on a petition urging Johnson to run for re-election, despite his military service. After

I had gathered 30,000 signatures, I went to Washington to help Lady Bird and O. J. Webber run Johnson's office. In June 1942, I too received my Navy commission, and went to war.

By the time I left the NYA my salary had inched up to $200 a month. Not much money, even in those days. However, during my four years with the NYA, I made a wealth of contacts: Jessie Kellam, Sherman Birdwell, Bill Deason, Harvey Payne, Mac DeGeurin, Fenner Roth, Sidney Hughes, C. P. Little, Harold Green, and many others— men I worked with all my life.

But I never had as unconventional a first meeting with any of them as I had with Lyndon Johnson!

Five

Handsome Harry

Roy Keaton, from Weatherford, Texas, became active in Lions International in 1934. It wasn't long before Roy was Special Representative of Lions International—one of the organization's top posts—and traveled all over the world on Lion business.

I knew Roy because he began visiting the Lions Club of Austin during the forties, which is when I became a Lion. At that time, the Austin Lions Club consisted of about 250 of Austin's most prominent young men. When he was in Austin, Roy stayed at either the Driskill Hotel or the Stephen F. Austin Hotel.

The Driskill Hotel's barbershop was run by mild-mannered Harry Reasonover. Harry was one of the most popular barbers in town, and the Driskill's Barbershop was *the* place to go. While you got your hair cut, you caught up on local news and gossip.

Barber Harry was a bashful man in his sixties. He was a kind, sweet man and, compared to us young Lions, somewhat straight-laced. One of Harry's customers, whenever he came to town, was Roy Keaton. Harry and Roy became fast friends, and in the process Roy learned that Harry was easily embarrassed, but also that he liked to be kidded.

So as Keaton traveled around the country and overseas on Lion business, he began writing and mailing penny postcards to Reasonover at the Driskill. The cards were gently risqué. They never crossed the line, but with double entendres and dumb jokes usually suggested sex.

From 1942 to 1949, Keaton sent almost fifty cards from all over the world to Harry at the Driskill Hotel. The cards were usually addressed to "Handsome Harry" or "Ze Cute Barber" and were always signed "Fifi." The cards maintained the fiction that Handsome Harry was a suave rogue and Fifi a sexy innocent, trying—not always successfully—to maintain her virtue and be true to Harry.

One of the earliest cards to arrive at the Driskill was dated October 28, 1942: "My friend Lulu says that a Necking Party is one which lasts until somebody gives in, gives up, or gives out," "Fifi" wrote. "Sounds like one of our parties, doesn't it, Harry? Also, Lulu says a Cafeteria Kiss is one where everything's in reach and you just help yourself."

Harry couldn't wait to get cards like this and show them to his customers. He would prop the card on the shelf in front of the chair that held hair oils and brushes. When you came in for a haircut or a shave, Harry would say, "I got another card from Fifi." We fellows all knew to inquire about Fifi.

In November 1948, Fifi wrote from Charlotte, North Carolina, with the recent Presidential election in mind: "Now that the election is over, I feel so sorry for Governor Dewey. He had his eye on the White House for 8 years. But Harry Truman seems to have something besides his EYE on it."

By today's standards the cards were tame, but fifty years ago they were naughty enough to be confined to our all-male barbershop. Sometimes the front of the card was a picture of a half-naked woman, hands strategically placed, or a woman bending over, exposing a lot of panty. Dogs and fireplugs were popular; on the cover of one card a cartoon shows a car mechanic telling his female customer, "I don't see anything wrong with your rear end, Miss."

Today these cards would be unbearably corny and politically incorrect, but back then we thought they were the height of masculine sophistication. Whenever the postman delivered one, he would hand it to Harry and say, "I see you got another card from *that woman!*" Harry would grin and blush. Oh, that madcap Fifi!

In 1947 Fifi wrote from San Francisco: "I wish you were in sunny

California with me. I would take you out under an orange tree and let you have all you could knock off." From Paris in 1948: "My boy friend has been ill. He went to see a doctor and the doctor told him to take a cold bath every day and he would feel rosy all over. My boy friend says he plans to feel Rosy even *before* he takes his bath."

And from Ontario, June 24, 1948: "The absent-minded professor in our girls' school kissed all of his students good-bye and then gave his young wife a thorough examination."

These cards are probably valuable now. They're posted with antique stamps from all over the world, but they're valuable to me for sentimental reasons because I remember Harry and Roy, and the boys at the Driskill barbershop. They remind me of the days when I was young and irreverent, with a head of pomaded black hair, and life stretched ahead of me like a series of penny postcards from exotic places. When he received one, Harry felt like a playboy instead of a bashful barber. The cards were more than a joke to Roy; they were his unique way of keeping in touch with one of his favorite Lions Clubs.

Roy Keaton eventually became Director General of Lions International, and retired from the organization in 1961. Handsome Harry died in 1963. His postcard collection, wrapped with a rubber band, passed to his son-in-law, Larry Meriage, who showed it to me. The cards, yellowing and dog-eared now, still make me laugh.

The Driskill Hotel's barbershop was a sort of men's club where without paying dues we hung around, picked up tips on how to dress and act, and talked jobs, politics, and women. Places like that no longer exist, but they were a rite of passage and a lot of fun to my generation.

I can almost hear Harry saying, "You'll never guess what Fifi's up to now."

Sugar and Jake, Long Beach,
California, Summer 1945.

Six

The Navy Years

In May 1942, six months after Pearl Harbor, I received a probationary commission in the Navy and was sent to the U.S. Naval Reserve Midshipmen's School, Northwestern University, Chicago, for three months' training. When the United States entered the war in December, I had been unable to get a commission because I had a malocclusion (a badly aligned bite) and an ulcer. But a few months into the war, they would take just about anybody that breathed. At Northwestern University, I had to pass class instruction and prove I was physically fit in order to become an officer. Becoming an officer was important, because with the war spreading on all fronts, it was only a matter of time before I was drafted.

The Navy's goal was to take a green candidate and turn him into an officer as quickly and as efficiently as possible. Guys like me were called "ninety-day wonders." In Chicago, I lived with a hundred other ninety-day wonders in Tower Hall, an old hotel which had been converted into a dormitory. During the day I studied navigation, gunnery, and seamanship with the intent to become Ensign Pickle. Probably because I hadn't taken much advanced math at the university, navigation, or "shooting a star"—finding your ship's position based on your relation to the stars—gave me the most trouble. Or maybe I had no sense of direction because I had grown up on that vast West Texas prairie.

I still have one of my textbooks, *Knight's Modern Seamanship*. On page 762, yellow with age, there's a series of photographs of one sailor cheerfully attempting to resuscitate the inert figure of another, captioned "Reviving the Apparently Dead."

I must not have spent *all* my time studying, because stuck between the pages, as though used as a bookmark, was a small formal card printed with the message "You and your party will oblige the management by leaving quietly." I can only surmise that other officer candidates and I partied heartily in some establishment—and were politely evicted.

At the end of my training, I used my ten days of leave—to get married! I had been dating Ella Nora "Sugar" Critz of Austin for over a year. From Chicago, I proposed to her over the phone. It was an impetuous step, but that's how it was in wartime. All around us, couples soon to be torn apart by war were getting married. Sugar's parents, Judge and Mrs. Richard Critz, printed formal wedding invitations which left the date blank, as was customary for war weddings. The date was filled in by hand at the last minute when the groom—in this case me—knew when he'd get leave.

As a wedding present, a group of twelve buddies, including Braniff Airways District Traffic Manager (later Braniff Airlines President) Bob Burck, bought me a one-way airline ticket from Chicago to Austin. Just so I didn't get too sentimental about their generosity, on September 18, 1942, Burck wrote, "I feel sure I can speak for each of them and say that . . . our motive . . . (is) to make it possible for you to be in Austin earlier, so we can deal you just that much more misery."

Sure enough, when I arrived in Austin, Joe Kilgore, Tom Beasley, Ed Syers, Mac DeGeurin, John Connally, and a dozen other old running buddies gave me a bachelor's party at the Driskill Hotel. After cocktails, they held a mock trial, enumerating my crimes against them, found me "guilty," and as punishment stripped me naked, doused me with mercurochrome, and bound me head to toe with surgical tape. I got all the tape off, but you could say that the wedding, two days later, was a sticky situation.

On September 29, 1942, Sugar and I got married in Austin's First Methodist Church—she in a white satin gown and I in a white summer uniform with an ensign's bar on my shoulder. Brother Joe was my best man and sister Judith was one of Sugar's four bridesmaids. We spent our wedding night at the Roosevelt Hotel in Waco, then took a Pullman for California. In California, we had a week before I shipped out. We spent two nights at the Biltmore Hotel in San Francisco and five nights at the Sir Frances Drake Hotel in Los Angeles—for a total of $46.11!

We said good-bye in San Francisco. Sugar took the Southern Pacific back to Austin, and I was sent to Women's Bay, Kodiak, Alaska, to report to my ship, the USS *St. Louis* (CL49). Aboard the converted troop ship USS *Denali*, I sailed up the Inland Passage, from Vancouver to Skagway. I stood on the deck, goggle-eyed at the scenery. As a boy raised in dry West Texas, I never knew such beauty existed, and I was stunned. Then and now, I think Alaska's Inland Passage is one of the most beautiful places on earth.

While en route, I learned that the *St. Louis* had already sailed for San Francisco. So I telegraphed Sugar. Happily, both of us headed back to San Francisco.

There, despite the fact that housing of any kind was nearly impossible to find, Sugar found a small bungalow in Villejo, about twenty-five miles outside San Francisco. We had a month's reprieve while the ship was outfitted. During the day I reported for duty; at night we dined and drank with other young couples on the brink of war. It was a gay time, not just because it was our honeymoon, but because that month's delay was stolen time, a delicious lull before the storm.

Just before Christmas 1942, I shipped out for real, and once again Sugar boarded a train for Texas. This time there was no reprieve. The USS *St. Louis* headed for the Solomon Islands in the Pacific. I watched as the big ship plowed those gray waters and thought, "This is it." One day I was a happy groom, the next I belonged to the Navy.

I didn't know it then, but during my three and a half years of service in the Navy, the only time I would get extended leave was the two or three times my ship docked for repairs. Each time, Sugar would jump on a train and meet me: twice in California and once in Philadelphia.

In the South Pacific, the *St. Louis'* home port was Espiritu Santo in the New Hebrides. I bunked in a tiny cabin on the main deck with C. L. "Barney" Lewis from Richmond, Virginia. While on board ship, we officers occasionally got a day of liberty. Most of the time we would head for the officer's club on Espiritu Santo, where they served rotgut whiskey flown in from Australia, or wherever the Navy could find it. It was understood that the Navy provided liquor for its fighting men, but it wasn't always good stuff like that in the States. Once in a while, the ship's doctor would sneak distilled alcohol out of sick bay, and in our cabins, we would cut it with fruit juice from the mess. It was a potent, dangerous brew, but we drank it. We were a lot more afraid of boredom and homesickness than of alcohol poisoning. Anyway, early in the war most of us still thought we were immortal.

Once when I had liberty, I went inland with other officers to a native village of bamboo huts. The islanders looked at us, and we looked at them. Somebody had propped a sun-bleached skull against a post. We gave the villagers gum, cigarettes, and candy bars, and they posed for pictures with us. Another officer took a picture of me pretending to drink from a coconut. The islanders were small; most didn't come up to my collarbone. Smallest of all was the wizened old chief, with skin as dark and wrinkled as an elephant's hide. Except for a thong and a Sam Browne belt, he was naked. The bare-breasted women were gaunt, with missing teeth. During the war, a lot of myths sprang up about lithesome South Sea women, but the women on Espiritu Santo just looked as if they had been worked half to death. I saw the little grass shack, but unlike the popular song, I didn't want to go back.

In August 1943, in the Solomon Islands off New Georgia Island, in the Battle of Kula Gulf, the USS *St. Louis* was torpedoed, but didn't sink. When I was studying *Knight's Modern Seamanship* in Chicago, the fine points of ship construction had escaped me, but in the Pacific, the importance of water-tight compartments became instantly apparent.

After the Battle of Kula Gulf I had a new attitude about the war. Looking back, I would call it an epiphany. Then, it was the Moment Everything Became Clear.

I was standing on the deck of the ship one night, watching a firefight created by the big guns of half a dozen battleships and cruisers firing almost simultaneously. Above the dark water, it was bright enough to read a newspaper. There was, I realized, danger both above and below the surface. I suddenly thought, "Hey! You could get killed out here! *I* could get killed out here!"

That was the first time I realized my own mortality. Before, I had felt relatively complacent aboard that big, armored ship. Suddenly I realized we were little boats floating in a very big bathtub—and somebody was always going to be throwing rocks in the tub. After Kula Gulf, the USS *St. Louis* limped back to Tulagi, a harbor in the New Hebrides, and finally to Long Beach, California, for repairs.

Before reporting for my next assignment, I got over two weeks' leave, enough time to get to Austin. While there, I spoke at a war bond rally at House Park. There were a lot of dignitaries at the rally: Governor Coke Stevenson, Congressman Lyndon Johnson, Senator Tom Connally, Austin Mayor Tom Miller, even film star Robert Taylor and boxer Jack Dempsey. Sugar was thrilled, because we got to ride into the stadium in a caravan of twenty-five cars, while six military transport planes flew overhead in salute. House Park was filled to capacity. It was a fine day to be young and part of the war effort—*and* safe at home on leave.

Along with the dignitaries, Major (later, Congressman) Joe Kilgore and I were asked to speak because we were local boys fresh from the fighting. Johnson, who was instrumental in organizing the rally, understood the importance of local heroes to the folks back home. I scribbled some notes on the back of my program and, nervous as hell, stood at the podium in my white uniform and made a short speech, one of my first. I expressed appreciation for the show of support, and ended with, "I say yes! This is worth fighting for!" I don't know how inspirational I was, but on the other hand, I didn't do anything to disgrace myself.

Before I left San Diego, I received new orders. I was assigned to the USS *Miami* (CL89). The ship, a brand new light cruiser, was under construction at the Cramp Shipbuilding Company in Philadelphia. While we waited six months for the ship to be commissioned, Sugar and I lived at the Walnut Park Plaza Apartments in Philadelphia, along with three or four other officers assigned to the ship and their wives. Every morning, we officers reported to Cramp's Shipyard, where we drilled our crew, held seminars, checked equipment, and readied the ship for service.

Back at the Walnut Park Plaza, the wives would get together. They would shop for and fix dinner, since we came home every night. They attended events for officer's wives. Some women had small children, so everybody took turns watching the kids. There was a Chinese laundry in the basement of the building. One day one of the wives mistakenly left her diaphragm in the pocket of her bathrobe when she sent it to the laundry. The Chinese counter man called to say they had found object in madam's kimono—please, nice lady, come get it. Nice lady was mortified, and would not. But Sugar thought it was hilarious, marched down, and retrieved it.

The USS *Miami* was commissioned on December 28, 1943, in the Philadelphia Navy Yard. The captain was John G. Crawford. It was a state-of-the-art ship, with twelve six-inch and twelve five-inch guns, and 20 and 40 mm. anti-aircraft batteries. Fortunately for me, the *Miami* also had modern sick bay and operating facilities.

I served on the *Miami* for the rest of the war.

After we sailed out of Philadelphia Harbor, the *Miami* headed for a "shakedown" cruise in the Caribbean. A shakedown was a floating test drive—it was how the crew got familiar with the ship, and got the kinks out. Somehow, the ship cruised too close to a sandbar and ran aground. That's when I was introduced to the old Naval practice of "sallying." Every seaman lined up on the deck of the ship. From the loudspeaker an order was barked: "All hands to Port!" and en masse hundreds of men rushed to the other side of the ship. Then the loudspeaker barked, "All hands to Starboard!" and we ran back to the first side. We did this over and over in the hot Caribbean sun.

This exercise was supposed to rock the ship, freeing it from the sand, but the ship wouldn't budge. After running like squirrels over the deck for an hour, we were sweaty and tired. We thought the whole business was silly. One by one, all hands started slipping below deck. It wasn't long before there were only a few men standing on deck. Captain Crawford—"the old man"—saw this, and he was fit to be tied. Again, the loudspeaker summoned all hands on deck, but this time only a few hands reported.

Finally, a tug had to be called to pull the *Miami* free, and a ship's inquiry was called soon after that. We figured we were safe; they couldn't court-martial everybody! As usual in official inquiries, a "culprit" had to be found, and one was. It ended up being the navigator, who wasn't in the conning tower when we ran aground.

Like the *St. Louis*, the *Miami* cruised the South Pacific. Most of the time, we escorted battleships or carriers, but we engaged in surface action, too—firing guns from our deck. We fired at kamikaze aircraft, shooting several down. Fortunately for us, the kamikazes were more interested in big game—the carriers—than in us. In fact, it got to be a joke with the carriers we escorted that the enemy avoided us so assiduously that the *Miami* must have a big banner lying on the deck that said "THIS WAY TO THE CARRIER," and an arrow pointed in their direction.

The *Miami* had its share of close calls. Once we were hit dead center by a torpedo, but it was a dud! All over the ship, men saw and heard it coming in, and the cry went up . . . "Here it comes! Here it comes!" And then, my God, it didn't explode.

Another time a torpedo did hit, blowing off our bow as far back as the twentieth frame (rib) of the ship. Again, we didn't sink because we had water-tight compartments. In one year we survived three hurricanes, with winds between 80 and 150 miles per hour. The waves were so enormous that sometimes we would have a roll of over 80 degrees. I'll tell you, a 10,000-ton cork rolling on its side is a stomach-upsetting experience! You feel it coming, and although your brain says you'll come upright again, your gut goes all the way down with the ship.

When we weren't engaged in battle, there was a lot of horseplay on the ship. Otherwise, boredom would drive you crazy. We had evening movies on the fantail of the ship. During the day we ate "geedunks," ice cream–like concoctions made of powdered milk. Considering the circumstances, our food was pretty good. A favorite prank was to drop a "gizmo"—a condom filled with water—into a man's pocket as he stood at attention, then slap it. He was forced to stand solemnly while a wet stain spread down his trousers. We thought that was hilarious. Ensign Fred Crow of Waco, Texas, was an easy target.

We got mail irregularly, depending on the location of the ship. When we were in a port like Espiritu Santo, mail arrived several times a week. But at sea, the only time we received mail was when a plane landed on a carrier nearby. Our outgoing letters piled up in the mail room. When we docked after weeks at sea, we would have a dozen letters to the same person waiting to go. My first Christmas on board ship I was given the responsibility of censoring outgoing mail. One old boy wrote his wife, "Today is Christmas. Even though we're in the South Sea, last night I hung up my stocking. Result? I lost my stocking!"

I wrote the folks back home and answered people who had written me. At Sugar's request, I traced my feet on brown butcher paper and mailed the outlines to her. She sent the crude pattern to Leddy's in San Angelo, where they hand-cut and stitched my first pair of boots, brown "Pee Wees" with cut-in heels and squared-off toes. I was the only man aboard the USS *Miami*—and possibly in the South Pacific—with cowboy boots. I still have them.

Sometimes, Sugar sent pralines from Lamme's Candies in Austin. My shipmates loved chewy PRA-lines, as they pronounced them. Pralines had a longer shelf life than fudge or cookies, and they didn't arrive smashed to pieces. They were so popular that whenever I was away from my cabin, guys would sneak in and "borrow" a few. Just as I had done with Mom's cookies at Little Campus, I hid the pralines in my foot locker, but in the South Pacific I didn't have an oiled rope or mousetrap to discourage culprits.

When I wasn't on duty, I spent a lot of time sitting around in the mess hall, smoking and drinking coffee. Our ship's doctor was Harold Williams, from Iowa and Texarkana, Texas. Harold told me that cigarettes and coffee weren't doing my ulcer any good and suggested I quit. He was right, and I did. When my appendix became infected, Harold took it out in sick bay's operating room. He administered a newfangled local anesthetic the Navy had just adopted, but when he started to cut, I jumped a couple of fathoms. Harold said mildly, "Can you feel that, Jake?" and when I assured him I could, he said, "Well, I declare. I'll just give you a little more juice," and calmly gave me another injection.

The day after my surgery, we got word that we were headed for the Sea of Japan, for possible engagement. The ship's sick bay was below deck. I made the fastest recovery in the history of medicine, and was back in my main deck cabin the next day!

After the war, I talked Harold into moving to Austin and setting up practice. He was our family doctor and my friend until his death forty years later.

Sitting around the mess hall with the other guys, I discovered something: G.I. Joes aren't the only servicemen who cuss the military. *All* branches of the service are cussed and discussed. Along with every sailor on board, I complained about the food, the mail service, the tedium, the shortage of hot water, the bureaucracy, the "old man," and the executive officers. In short, everything. But the truth was, I liked the Navy.

It was years later before I realized that the more you grumbled, the more afflicted, put upon, stalwart—in other words, special—you felt about your service. Aboard both ships I made friends like Harold Williams, Eli Schaffer, Eddie Collins, Fred Crow, Cam Brock, and Bill Ferguson that I kept for life. In general, I found the Navy to be responsive to its men. But three thousand miles from home, with time on our hands, we griped and boasted. We sank more ships in the barroom than in battle! Even today, we are self-appointed heroes and, like politicians, we speak highly of each other.

Life aboard a ship is a noisy place. Other than inside your head, there is very little privacy. Early on, you learn to make your peace with the confinement and uproar. But when the ship got orders to go to General Quarters in preparation for combat, *then* it got awfully quiet. To be honest, most of us were just plain scared. We had confidence in our ship and knew "it" couldn't happen to us, but still . . .

We would take our positions. In the quiet, you could hear men all over the ship whispering to each other: "What do you hear?" "How many ships have they got?" "Reckon this is part of the Tokyo Express?" As the minutes dragged by, somebody would say hopefully, "I hear they've changed direction."

One thing I never *did* hear during combat was "Let's get those SOBs!" We waited quietly, listening to our own heartbeat, and when action did come, there was no time to talk. Declarations of aggression came when the battle was over. On the way back to the port, men are as bold as hell!

My duty on board the USS *Miami* was to serve as a gunnery officer. At sea, officers took turns serving on deck, plotting a course, and steering the ship. I still had a lot to learn. The first time I shot the stars, my positioning placed the *Miami* near the South Pole! I was quickly transferred to the gun deck.

Sometimes I stood watch for Captain Crawford, who didn't believe in radar. What he did believe in was a man hanging like a figurehead from the bow of the ship! I never understood that. By the time I spotted the enemy, he would have been upon us—and I would have been squashed as flat as a sandwich. One winter during a shakedown cruise to Maine I stood in the wind for hours outside the conning tower, peering through binoculars, freezing to death. One watch, shipmate Eli Schaffer from Houston knew I was on duty. He called me from the warm engine room and told me how much he was enjoying his cup of coffee.

But I got even with Schaffer. A few days later, when we were called to General Quarters and I knew Eli was in the engine room, I called and told him a torpedo had just been sighted: it was closing in fast on the engine room! Eli didn't even hang up. He discovered sudden and pressing business above deck.

When Schaffer found out I was behind that prank, he was steamed. The next watch he had a call in the engine room: "Full steam ahead!" was the order. "Aw, go to Hell, Pickle!" he barked.

It was Captain Crawford—who had his *own* suggestion about what Schaffer should do.

Another time, a new ensign, fresh from the Naval Academy, was shocked at how informally Captain Ferguson, who headed the Marine contingent aboard ship, ran his watch. The new officer asked permission to speak to Ferguson "man-to-man," and it was granted.

"Sir, I think you run a very poor watch," the young officer blurted. Ferguson thought that over. Then he said, "Man-to-man—fuck you!"

Often at night in the South Pacific, when I was on duty standing watch in the directory, the five-inch gun turret high atop the ship, I would gaze awestruck at the panorama above me, horizon to horizon inky black with a million pinpoints of light. I had never experienced such a feeling of insignificance. We are only a little speck in the universe, and not for long.

During those moments of solitude, the words from the second verse of "Home, Home on the Range" came to me. You don't hear the second verse much, but it goes:

How often at night
When the Heavens are bright
With the light from the glittering stars
Have I stood there amazed
And asked as I gazed
If their glory exceeds that of ours?

Sometimes I wondered if the Japanese, my unseen enemy in the soft dark night, had similar thoughts. Was the glory that exceeded all of us the same glory?

At times like these my thoughts would turn to home—to Sugar, Mom and Pop, the university, my friends. To the young man I was before the war. I yearned for these and other things so strongly I could cry. Looking up at those stars, I prayed and made myself a promise. If I ever got back home, I would try to do something important and good. I didn't know what, but I promised myself I would find it—and then I would do it.

If only I could survive the war!

All around me, men were thinking similar thoughts, though we rarely shared them. If you dwelled on your loneliness or fear, it drove you crazy. Most of us had boarded the *St. Louis* and the *Miami* young and green. We matured in a few months. We saw first hand that life was short, and all that stood between you and the beautiful nothingness of the stars was a few seconds' luck.

The *Miami* weathered its third hurricane in July 1945. But it cracked the bow of the ship, and we had to return to San Francisco for repairs. About the time we docked, we heard about Hiroshima, and knew the war was almost over.

Sugar met me in Long Beach. We expected—hoped—that I would be discharged immediately along with many of my shipmates. But the Navy discharged men according to a complicated system based on the time you had served, the miles you had sailed in which war zones, and so on. You needed sixty points to be discharged, and I had fifty-nine! Moreover, by this time I was an "Officer of the Deck Underway," qualified to navigate a ship at sea.

I had finally figured out how to shoot a star well enough that they actually needed me.

So, with one point to go, I kissed Sugar good-bye and set sail for Okinawa. Somewhere in the middle of the ocean I earned my sixtieth point, but had to wait until I boarded another ship returning to San Francisco before I could be discharged. As fast as I could get my papers processed, I grabbed a ride to Texas.

I was discharged from the Navy as a Lieutenant Senior Grade, just a few days short of being a Lieutenant Commander. They told me if I stayed, I would receive my promotion immediately. But I wanted to go home! I didn't know yet what I wanted to do, but the same way I had known at the university that my future wasn't in the practice of law, I knew it wasn't in the Navy, either. And yet, three and a half years and two ships after I joined up, I *still* liked the Navy. The Navy was good to me.

In September 1945, almost as quickly as I had begun Naval service, I left active duty and started a new life. But although I didn't know it at the time, I had *already* started a new life, figuratively and literally. Before I had shipped out for Okinawa, during our reunion in California, Sugar had gotten pregnant. Our daughter, Peggy, was born six months after I got home.

Fifty years and three months later, in June 1994, I was part of a Congressional delegation to ceremonies commemorating D-Day in Normandy. When I was first elected to Congress in 1963, it seemed as if half the members of the House and Senate had seen service in World War II, either overseas or in the reserves. But by the time of the fiftieth anniversary commemoration, I was one of about two dozen World War II veterans still serving in Congress. Instead of a young warrior, I was one of the fast-disappearing old guard.

In the fifty years since I had left the Navy, I had been to Europe several times, and had even visited Normandy. During World War II, I had served in the Pacific, not the European Theater. So I thought I was prepared to go back. I wasn't.

As I surveyed row after row of pristine white crosses, I was struck with the sudden, awful realization of the millions of young men and women, like myself, who had died during the time I served in the South

Pacific. I survived; they had not. During the war, most of the time I was so convinced of my own invulnerability, it seemed incredible to me that so many others, equally vital, had died while I was shooting stars and eating geedunks in the South Pacific. How could that have happened?

When young men—and today, young women—go off to war, despite their fears, they really don't think anything is going to happen to them. Here was proof that it *had* happened, and to millions. That simple realization hit me hard, and humbled me.

Before his death in 1970, one of my good friends was Earl Rudder, a Texas General Land Commissioner and later President of Texas A&M University. Rudder was one of the great heroes of D-Day. He had led his famous Ranger Battalion ashore and up the cliffs at Pointe du Hoc in Normandy. But although Rudder was one of the most decorated men of World War II, he didn't talk about it much. Sometimes when we sat around drinking beer, we would get to talking about the war, and Rudder would shake his head and say, "It was rough. Rough!" Of course, I knew what he had done, but he never went into detail. Not until June 1994, fifty years after Rudder led that charge, when I stood at the base of those terrible cliffs and looked up at those sheer rock walls, did I realize how rough it really *was*. I don't know how Earl Rudder found the courage to do what he did. Today, a part of me can't comprehend surviving three and a half years as a floating target in the Pacific. Somehow, I emerged with my humor, optimism, ambition—and hide—intact.

It's only later that you don't know how you accomplished a hard thing. When you're young, you think you can do anything, and often you can.

"*The KVET Boys*," 1946.
BACK, LEFT TO RIGHT:
John Connally, Ed Clark, Ed Syers, Jake Pickle.
FRONT, LEFT TO RIGHT:
Sherman Birdwell, Willard Deason, Jessie Kellam, Bob Phinney.

Seven

The KVET Boys

After the end of World War II, soldier boys, sailor boys, and flyboys came home by the thousands, and I was one of them. While stationed in the Pacific, my shipmates and I had talked for hours about what we would do "after"—after nobody was firing torpedoes at us, after we went home to our families. But although I did my share of talking, I had never come to a firm conclusion. Sometimes I thought about going back to law school. But I had been a poor law student, and now I had a wife to support. If I didn't have the temperament for a career in law, I didn't have the money or time to prepare for one, either.

The Austin I returned to in November 1945, with a population of approximately 110,000, was a sleepy little Southern town beginning a postwar expansion. Austin was home to the University of Texas, the State Capitol, and recently named Bergstrom Air Force Base. Servicemen came home, enrolled in college, got jobs, had babies, and scrambled for housing. The boom was on.

Since I had gotten home a few months late, a lot of jobs were already gone, filled by returning servicemen. John Connally, among others, urged me to go to work for Austin radio station KTBC, 590 on the dial, the station owned by Congressman Lyndon Johnson and Lady Bird. Connally said working for KTBC would be good experience."Besides," he said, "we're trying to get together a radio station of our own, and we want you to be a part of it."

By "we" he meant a group of young men who were Johnson's friends and supporters, and with whom Johnson had worked in the past. After the war, Johnson liked the idea of "his boys"—men he could count on and trust—staying in Austin. We were a good group; he didn't want to see us split up and scattered all over the country. Johnson always looked at things for the long haul. In 1945 I was worrying about putting food on the table; Johnson was already thinking about future projects, deals, and races.

It was probably Johnson as much as anybody who thought up the idea of a another radio station in Austin. It might sound funny that he encouraged competition, but he knew that after the war, Austin would grow. It was inevitable that another radio station would join the two already broadcasting.

In 1945, KTBC's only competitor was radio station KNOW (1490), but Johnson got along well with KNOW's owners, Charlie Woodson and Wendell Mayes, and he liked it that way. Johnson's reasoning was that he'd rather do business with friends than enemies. As long as nobody stepped on his toes!

Johnson thought that if "his boys" founded a third radio station, they could stay in Austin, get in on a good thing, and be available when he needed them. Politically and financially, it made sense.

By the time I got home, Johnson had already convinced Connally that this was the thing to do. Johnson promised to use his connections in Washington to help us get a license.

I didn't need much encouraging. I liked selling ads for KTBC, but I liked the idea of being a radio station owner better! Also, by this time Sugar and I were expecting a baby. Suddenly I was a family man. So I said yes.

In addition to Connally and me, our group of "boys" included Ed Syers, Jessie "J. C." Kellam, Sherman Birdwell, Willard "Bill" Deason, Ed Clark, Bob Phinney, Walter Jenkins, and Merrill Connally, John's brother. John Connally, Syers, Kellam, Birdwell, Deason, and I had served in the Navy; Phinney and Jenkins were Army, Merrill Connally was a Marine. All of us except Clark, who served in the National Guard

Reserve, were just back from overseas. Another veteran, Joe Kilgore, considered investing in KVET, but decided to practice law instead.

Through Johnson, we contacted Leonard Marks, a Washington attorney who specialized in issues before the Federal Communications Commission and who did all the legal communications work for the Johnson family. Marks helped us prepare an application for a license with the FCC. Filing the application was time-consuming and tedious. Once the application was filed, all we could do was wait. In the meantime, we discovered that a group of investors from San Antonio had applied for the same radio band frequency. It became a hot contest to see who would get the license first.

While we sweated it out, we thought about a name for the station. All sorts of call letters were kicked around, but none seemed right. Oddly enough, I think it was the manager of KNOW, Hardy Harvey, who came up with the answer. He said, "You guys are all veterans. Why don't you call yourself KVET? It's got a ring to it, and anything having to do with veterans is popular now." We liked that, and the name stuck.

When our application for a license was approved, we set about finding a location. We negotiated a lease with Austin businessman Dewey Bradford for an abandoned warehouse at 113 West 8th, in back of the old "Shot Tower," a landmark 1866 building, allegedly the site of clandestine gunpowder production after the Civil War. The Shot Tower and our adjacent warehouse quickly became known as "Bradford's Alley."

We were young and cocky. The world was ours! We decided that we didn't want just a station, we wanted a *beautiful* station, one that was the envy of Texas broadcasting. We employed a sound expert, Professor C. P. Bonar, to transform our old warehouse into a modern studio.

Upstairs, on the warehouse's main floor, were KVET's offices. Downstairs were the turntables, mikes, and consoles. Furnishing the office was fairly simple, because all we needed were desks, telephones, and typewriters. Most of our money went into the studios.

KVET actually had three studios: A, B, and C. Studio A was by far the grandest. Professor Bonar constructed what he called "rolling pillows," curved mahogany walls that could be moved around to accommodate a full-size orchestra or country-western band. Bonar installed thick carpet and a sound-absorbent ceiling. In the middle of the studio stood a magnificent black Steinway grand piano. Studio A, which was described in an opening-week article in the *Austin American* as "streamlined in soothing gray and modernistic in design," was where we took dignitaries and people we wanted to impress.

Studio B was smaller, with an announcer's booth and a couple of chairs at one end. This was our workhorse studio, where most of our broadcasting originated. Studio C was no bigger than a closet. It was called the "stand-up booth" because there wasn't room to sit down. You talked into a mike hanging from the wall.

Connally bought land "way out north"—near the present-day intersection of Balcones and 2222—for the station's transmitter. We razzed him because we thought he had paid too much, but Connally said, "You wait. Someday this land will be worth more than the station."

We spent way too much money fixing up the studios, but we were dreaming big. Big meant modern! First-class! Progressive! The money for all this remodeling came from us shallow-pocket investors. Each of us put in approximately $5,000, which entitled that shareholder to 5 percent of KVET's stock. The exception was Connally, who owned 51 percent. I think Connally borrowed most of his $40,000 share from the Capital National Bank.

I borrowed $3,000 of my share from my father-in-law, Judge Richard Critz. Sugar and I had saved the rest out of my Navy pay. In 1945, you could buy a brand new home for $10,000, so that $5,000 investment seemed like a fortune.

Some of the KVET boys were investors only; some of us became employees of the new station. Connally was general manager. I was sales manager. Bob Phinney was a salesman and business manager. Ed Syers was news and program director. Merrill Connally was in sales.

This meant the station had to make enough money to pay our salaries. We agreed to take small salaries for the first six months, until the station made a profit. And it was a *small* salary! I brought home $250 a month. By the fall of 1946, baby Peggy had arrived. Two hundred fifty dollars a month didn't go a long way toward feeding a family of three.

But we got a break for opening day—October 1, 1946. There was a hot National League playoff going on between the St. Louis Cardinals and the Brooklyn Dodgers, to determine who would play the Boston Red Sox in the World Series. KVET, which was affiliated with the Mutual Broadcasting System, was going to broadcast the World Series. So we decided to take advantage of the enormous interest in the game by opening KVET on the first day of the playoffs. In those days before television or professional football, baseball was the national passion. We knew every sports fan in Austin would immediately discover 1300 on the dial.

We placed ads in the *Austin American* telling people to tune to KVET for game coverage. The night before our grand opening, we KVETs worked late at the station painting, hanging pictures, and laying carpet. We were on the carpet even *before* the station opened!

We had agreed to go on the air at 6 A.M. sharp. Mayor Tom Miller had accepted our invitation to share the mike with Connally and many of us owners. We intended to cut up and put on a little show.

But the night before, as we left the station dirty and exhausted, I had made a wager with Connally, who was not a morning person, that he would oversleep. Sure enough, the next morning, Connally came stumbling in twenty minutes late—and was greeted by Mayor Miller. So that first day, KVET didn't go on the air until 6:30 A.M.

Not long after our grand opening, *Broadcasting* magazine put our picture on the cover. In the picture, eight of the ten KVET boys faced the camera in uniform, as serious as hanging judges, perhaps thinking of the money we had poured into the station.

Those early days were tough for KVET, because we were constantly foraging for new advertisers. We had made a gentleman's agreement with Johnson that we wouldn't go after any of "his" advertisers; we had to find our own. KNOW's ad salesmen, Chester Sykes and Marion "Pappy" Coleman, were tough competitors. The three stations were scrambling for slices of a very small pie.

Some of the programs KVET offered were staples: national news with Fulton Lewis Jr., Gabriel Heatter, and Cedric Foster; the soap opera *Queen for a Day*; Buck Rogers and Tom Mix for the kids; *The Shadow Knows* mystery program for the whole family, and of course, music, music, music.

I still have a 1946 newspaper ad which lists the station's music programming for one day. From sign-on at 6 A.M. until sign-off at midnight it lists in sequence: Western music, dance music, march music, variety music, sweet music, string music, waltz music, favorite music, swing music, serenade music, luncheon music, Hawaiian music, Latin American music, dinner music, and something called light music. Just in case the listener hadn't had enough music, several categories were repeated during the day! I suspect a lot of it was Tommy Dorsey playing everything under the sun, but every type of music got a separate billing. We had the whole day to fill!

In order to attract new listeners—and advertisers—we had to think up new programs. We began a Saturday night dance program, *The 1300 Club*. People would phone in a request for a song, and we would play it. We thought it would be a cheap show to produce, because our only expense would be new 78 rpm records, but we were wrong. It cost peace of mind.

The 1300 Club became a favorite with bobby-soxers. At first we were delighted, but not for long. Every Saturday night, as soon as *The 1300 Club* came on the air, the kids would pile in cars and head for the station. We made the mistake of letting a few of them make requests on the air, and that started the deluge. *The 1300 Club* became a mob scene.

We KVETs were forced to stand guard in the lobby. As the requests came in, we would carry the scraps of paper to Fred, seated at a turntable in Studio B. Hank Williams was a favorite, of course. I remember a couple of other songs that were popular: "Cold Stone Dead in the Market" was a favorite with lovers nursing a broken heart; "Open the Door, Richard" was a novelty tune. Kids loved to yell out its title refrain at the top of their lungs, while knocking on the nearest hard surface. "Open the Door, Richard" made your head ache.

Finally, *The 1300 Club* became a victim of its own popularity. So many people—mostly teenagers—were showing up at the station that we had to draft our wives to come down and help out. So there were Sugar and I, John and Nellie Connally, Ed and Maggie Syers, and Bob and Helen Phinney patrolling the lobby of KVET every Saturday night, trying to keep order. After a while, our wives, who had seen us put in twelve-hour days all week, revolted. On Saturday night, they wanted to dress up and go out. *The 1300 Club* wasn't what they had in mind!

The 1300 Club had a lot of young fans, but the fans had even less money than we did. So we announced to our listeners that we were "revamping" the show. The truth was, it vamped us. We took it off, and we never brought it back.

I still have three boxes of old KVET records, which during the last fifty years I've moved all the way to Washington, D.C., then back to Texas when I retired from Congress. Although I'm too sentimental to let them go, I'm afraid that if I play them, a hundred kids in jalopies will appear at my front door.

Another program KVET initiated was *Noche de Fiesta*, which was aimed at Austin's Hispanic community. *Noche de Fiesta* featured Lalo Campos as our announcer. Each night after the news, Lalo played Spanish music for an hour. We didn't make much money on *that* program, either, but we got a big listening share of East Austin. I think *Noche de Fiesta* was the first regular radio program in Austin for and about Hispanics.

KVET covered a lot of baseball games, because sports events were popular with advertisers. Austin's minor league baseball team was the Austin Senators. We'd send our commentator, "Dr. Hepcat," to cover the games. Dr. Hepcat was a black man named Albert Lavada Durst who had a lingo all his own. Dr. Hepcat called a southpaw pitcher "a sand man," and said runners "*sluuuud* inta' third." A lot of people listened to Senator games solely for the pleasure of hearing Dr. Hepcat say, "Cool Papa Chaney walkin' to the mound, catchin' is Big King Kong Jones." White announcers didn't talk like that!

When Dr. Hepcat said, "Here we are, in the coooool of the evenin' . . . ," he had all the hush-voiced drama of a host of grand opera. He was as good an entertainer as he was an announcer, and he became famous all over Austin. Durst also announced *Rosewood Ramble*, the first radio program in Austin (and, Durst thought, the South) hosted by a black D.J.

Dr. Hepcat's popularity led to trouble. Some whites resented his success; some blacks thought his jive talk was an insult to their race. So Durst went to Connally and offered to resign. Connally said forget it, that if he'd wanted a proper professor for an announcer, he'd have gone to the university and gotten one! Dr. Hepcat stayed.

KVET's format was simple: music, news, and sports. One of our announcers was Dave Smith. Our main announcers were Bonner McLane and Fred Coleman. Fred gave air time to new musical groups like the Geezinslaw Brothers. KVET got national news from UPI and AP wires. We played a little Big Band and a *lot* of country-western; Fred Coleman loved country music.

KVET signed on the air at 6 A.M. and signed off at midnight. Our network affiliate, Mutual Broadcasting, fed us national news three times a day and contributed occasional programs. It was up to us to fill the rest of the time. We filled it with local news, music, baseball, and special events. When Purina hired Eddie Arnold to open an Austin store, we were there.

To everyone's dismay, KVET's elaborate, expensive Studio A had poor acoustics. The big room had an echo. Few bands or orchestras played in the studio—we didn't have the money to hire them—so our movable walls rarely moved. Other than sports events, KVET's much-anticipated live programming usually consisted of the announcer alone at his mike.

None of us KVETs did much announcing. I read a few bulletins on the air, but I didn't have a "radio" voice; none of us did. In addition to Lalo Campos, Fred Coleman, Bonner McLane, and Dave Smith, another of our announcers, Stuart Long, was news director. Stuart was a slow-talking liberal Democrat. He was an able, courageous journalist, but he was fond of reading the local news, then editorializing. He'd say something like, "Well, I hear old (substitute the name of an Austin pillar) is buying a building downtown. We know where that money came from, don't we?" Stuart frequently put a spin on things, and when he spun, it was always to the left.

Often, when Stuart read the news, the phones would ring like crazy—and it *wasn't* good news calling. He was married to Emma Long (later, the first woman elected to Austin's City Council), whom I called Booger Red because of her fiery hair and temperament. Emma was a liberal Democrat too and later became one of Austin's best civic leaders. I spent half the time laughing at Stuart's outrageous on-the-air comments, and the rest of the time placating his victims.

As ad salesman, my job was to solicit business. I believe I physically

called on every business in Austin that didn't already advertise on
KTBC. I learned quickly who was a good prospect and who wasn't.
Beer distributors, jewelry and furniture stores bought ads; grocery stores
didn't. A regular thirty-second spot cost $2.10; a prime-time spot (brack-
eting a newscast) cost $3.50. Time signals—as in "KVET time is 9:35,
courtesy of Joe Koen Jewelers"—sold for $1.50. Occasionally, we would
offer special rates for baseball games or holiday programs. Specials were
$30.00 for a fifteen-minute segment. Specials didn't make us rich, but
they paid bills.

Across Lake Austin, George Hatley was developing Rollingwood.
He bought a few ads on our *Evening Classic* radio show from KVET
salesman Fleetwood Richards (a few years later, Richards sold this
popular program to the real estate firm Nash Phillips Copus). Hatley
tried to work a deal with KVET, trading undeveloped Rollingwood
lots for ad time. But KVET needed cash as much as Hatley did, so we
turned him down. That's one of our business decisions I try not to
think about.

Once I sold a series of ads to Leonard Karotkin—pronounced "Ka-
ROT-kin"—the owner of Karotkin's Furniture at Congress and 5th. In
those days, a merchandiser could gauge the effectiveness of his advertising almost immediately, depending on how many people appeared in
his store the same day he advertised on KVET. I personally assured
Leonard that his upcoming Saturday sale would make him rich. With
his ads running every few minutes, how could he miss?

That Saturday I was at home when the phone rang. It was Leonard,
and he sounded irritated. "Pickle," he croaked into the receiver, "are you
listening to your station?" I had to admit, I was not. "Well, you turn the
damn thing on," he growled; "then you call me back!"

I flipped on the radio dial. Our announcer, who was new to Austin,
was in the middle of an ad extolling the virtues of "Carrot-kin Furniture." As instructed by me, he was dutifully repeating "Carrot-kin" every
few seconds, to reinforce name recognition. Hastily, I called the station
and set him straight.

It took me a lot of cups of coffee and jokes with Leonard Karotkin
before I got *his* business again.

Being a radio executive was exciting, but gradually it became apparent that none of us could raise a family on what we were taking home. Part of it was the competition for ads. This was before national brands bought much local radio time. We had to survive on local business, and there wasn't enough to go around. Later, when the Korean War started, the nation's economy got another kick. Also, Congress passed legislation giving greater tax breaks to advertisers. That's when local radio took off.

One by one, KVET's original investors left the station. Ed Syers was first, resigning to open his own advertising and public relations agency. Early in 1949, I joined Ed; together we founded Syers-Pickle & Winn, Inc. Since we KVETs had agreed in the beginning that if we left the station, we would sell our stock to another KVET, I sold my stock to John Connally.

Connally left KVET himself in August 1949 to join the Austin law firm of Powell, Wirtz & Rauhut and, not long after that, to become Johnson's administrative assistant in Washington.

When I left KVET, I left a part of my heart behind. Never again would I be starting out with so much youth, excitement, and confidence. Yet I left without hesitation, because I couldn't afford to stay. Like every other investor, I knew the station would make it big one day. I would have liked to keep my stock, but I needed the money so I could roll it into Syers-Pickle & Winn.

All the KVET boys went on to bigger things. John Connally became Governor of Texas and Secretary of the Navy and the U.S. Treasury. Ed Clark became Ambassador to Australia and a partner in the Austin law firm of Looney & Clark, later Clark, Thomas, Winters & Newton. After Syers-Pickle & Winn folded, Ed Syers became a newspaperman and novelist. Sherman Birdwell became part-owner of Cook Funeral Home in Austin and a Texas Employment Commissioner. Bill Deason was appointed to the Interstate Commerce Commission and later became its chairman. J. C. Kellam managed the Johnson family's financial interests, including KTBC-TV. Bob Phinney became Austin's U.S. Postmaster and director of the Internal Revenue Service, South Texas. Merrill Connally became a county judge and, in the 1990s, a television pitch man for cataract surgery. Walter Jenkins became LBJ's administrative assistant in Washington.

Over the years, I discovered that a lot of people thought KVET was owned or financed by Lyndon Johnson. That wasn't true. We ten veterans owned all KVET's stock, and struggled to keep the station afloat. Although without Johnson, there probably wouldn't have been a KVET, once it was established, he never interfered in our operations. He didn't mess with us, and we sure didn't mess with him. *Or his advertisers.*

In the 1950s, when then-station manager Bill Deason moved KVET's transmission tower from north Austin to Westlake Hills, the sale of the old Balcones pad site made the station a lot of money. Connally's prediction came true.

Bradford's Alley no longer exists. The Capital National Bank, which owned the property at the time, razed the historic structure without warning one Saturday in 1974. Today the site of so many dreams and so much music and laughter is a parking lot.

KVET-AM and its partner station, KASE-FM, moved to 705 North Lamar in 1969. For over a decade, KVET-KASE has been rated by Arbitron as the most-listened-to station in Austin, thriving on a format of talk radio and country-western music. Today, the station, managed by Ron Rogers, is owned by Ann and Roy Butler. Together, they've put KVET on the "Glory Road." It's one of the best country-western stations in America. Fred Coleman would be pleased.

But it's still "my" KVET.

Dollars for Democrats

Throughout the 1950s, the Texas Democratic Party was embroiled in a bitter controversy to determine who controlled the party—conservative Democrats headed by Governors Allan Shivers and Price Daniel, or liberal Democrats such as Ralph Yarborough and labor leader Jerry Holleman. The controversy was so acrimonious that eventually even Speaker of the House Sam Rayburn and Senator Lyndon Johnson got involved.

Believe it or not, back then the split between conservative and liberal Democrats was as sharp a rivalry as exists today between Democrats and Republicans. In Texas, it wasn't just a matter of political philosophy; it was a matter of loyalty. Conservative Democrats like Johnson, Rayburn, Shivers, and others intended to maintain control of "their" party. Maintaining control was everything, because control meant votes, and votes meant legislation.

At the time, I was the Organizational Secretary of the State Democratic Executive Committee (SDEC), and in 1952 I represented Governor Shivers at the State Democratic Convention in Mineral Wells.

Governor Shivers decided he didn't want an Executive Committee dominated by liberal Democrats who would criticize him at every opportunity. As Governor, he thought he ought to be the titular head of the Democratic Party. He instructed me to remove from the SDEC nominations list people hostile to him. In the convention's committee on nominations in Mineral Wells, I did just that. It was dynamite!

Before the convention, in anticipation of opposition, I had called delegates I knew to be sympathetic to Shivers, but who were not planning to attend the convention. In their absence, I asked for and received over twenty-five proxies from chairmen of county delegations. So when I arrived at the convention, we had at least that many pro-Shivers votes already locked up.

As the convention roll call was made and the proxies were voted, it was like pouring gasoline on a smoldering fire. Anti-Shivers delegates on the floor howled in protest. It took us until 3 A.M. to quiet everybody down and end up with an Executive Committee that Shivers thought he could work with.

I think Mineral Wells was the first time an incoming Texas Governor had ruled that he would accept duly elected members of the SDEC only if they were friendly to him. Most of the members removed—and remember, they had been selected by their own caucuses—were furious. All sorts of rumors started flying—disgruntled delegates were going to break up the convention, or weren't going to let the convention adjourn. Then and now, I see their point.

Years later, the rules were changed to prevent advance nominations, but in the fifties, it was perfectly legal. Strong-armed and stressful, but legal.

Nineteen fifty-two was the same year I got involved in "The Port Arthur Story" controversy. Former assistant attorney general Ralph Yarborough ran in the Democratic primary for governor against Allan Shivers. I was selected as the statewide organizer for Shivers, and my advertising firm, Syers-Pickle & Winn, Inc., represented the Shivers campaign. Someone in the firm—not me; I wasn't that prescient—hit upon the idea to do a television spot for Shivers. That was bold strategy. Television was in its infancy then. Most Texas families didn't own a television set yet.

So the firm sent a small crew down to Port Arthur, Texas, which at the time was experiencing a crippling labor strike. Because Yarborough was aligned with labor, we thought publicity about the effects of the strike on Port Arthur's economy would damage Yarborough.

"The Port Arthur Story" was filmed early in the morning, I think around 6 A.M. I wasn't there because I was working on another project—it may have been Judge Meade Griffin's campaign for the Texas Supreme Court—but I knew the spot was being filmed. The finished ad showed a forlorn downtown Port Arthur, with only an occasional vehicle, closed stores, and a newspaper blowing down a lonely street. The voice-over talked about how labor's grip had paralyzed the city.

Sure it was deserted—it was 6 A.M.

The Shivers campaign aired the ad in only a few major Texas cities, but it was effective. Yarborough, who was a decent man, got mixed up in people's minds with Big Labor, outside interests, Communism, and God knows what all—just about every bugaboo that people worried about during those paranoid Red Menace years. Years later, Yarborough's people always complained that he would have been governor of Texas if it weren't for Jake Pickle. But the truth of the matter is that although it was my firm, it wasn't my spot. I got the credit and the blame.

Long before the televised Kennedy-Nixon debates, "The Port Arthur Story" showed me how powerful television would become in American politics. "The Port Arthur Story" left a bad taste in my mouth. When I was elected to public office myself, I never ran another negative, misleading campaign ad.

After 1952, the feud between Texas conservatives and liberals simmered and stewed. When Governor Price Daniel was elected to succeed Shivers, he continued Shivers' tradition of purging unfavorable SDEC members, although Daniel wasn't as ruthless as Shivers had been. By the 1954 State Democratic Convention, again in Mineral Wells, because I had been the governor's representative and done the dirty work at both conventions, I was dubbed "the hatchet man."

My hatchet-man reputation became such a joke in political circles that everybody thought up variations on the theme. Jack Dillard, who had been Allan Shivers' administrative assistant, had a two-line quip that became famous. Question: "Do you know Jake Pickle?" Answer: "No, but I suspect him."

Not long after the 1954 state Democratic convention, the National Democratic Committee, under the leadership of Paul McNutt of Indiana, proposed starting a nationwide program called Dollars for Democrats. McNutt wanted more people to participate in the democratic process, not just the usual party fat cats. The purpose was to get a little money from everybody, so all the contributors would feel that they had a direct part in the political machinery of the Democratic Party.

So the National Democratic Committee came to Texas and invited us to participate in the program. They made an attractive offer: money raised would be divided between the National Democratic Committee and the Texas Democratic Party, led by the SDEC. Well, this constituted a problem for us, because while we wanted to cooperate, we needed money to run our own organization. The SDEC had rented office space and hired two or three people, including me. I think we tried to negotiate a 50/50 split. But the National Democratic Committee said no, that wasn't appropriate for a national campaign. I think we finally settled on something like 75 percent to national, 25 percent to Texas.

I thought that was fair, and might even be the vehicle through which Texas conservatives and liberals could work together. I talked to some of the Democratic Party's liberal leaders, called the Democrats of Texas—the DOT—trying to get them to agree. Outspoken DOT members included Jerry Holleman, Alex Dickie, Fagan Dickson, John Cofer, Henry Holman, Creekmore Fath, and Frankie Randolph. In addition to being reluctant to see (their) liberal Democratic money going to conservative Democratic causes, DOT members were also angry about people who voted Democratic in the primary, then went into the voting booth in the November general election and voted whatever party they wished—meaning Republican. DOT urged passage of a "loyalty law." There was really no way to settle this issue (and forty years later there still isn't), but in those days it was *the* political topic in Texas.

At that time, the DOT state leader was Ralph Yarborough, who had been an opponent of both Shivers and Daniel. Yarborough and the DOT thought the SDEC, some of whom were DOT members, ought to speak for the Texas Democratic Party, and not just the governor.

Mrs. Frankie Randolph, an outspoken liberal Democrat from Houston, was helping finance the DOT, along with labor and other liberal "yellow-dog Democrats." Mrs. Randolph was a tough sister and a formidable opponent. She was committed to her cause and wasn't going to let anybody run over her.

When the DOT held their state caucus in 1956 to vote on the Dollars for Democrats proposal, the DOT didn't want any part of the proposed financial agreement. They didn't want to send their money to a National Democratic Committee unfavorable to them. They figured any money funneled to Texas would be controlled by Governor Daniel and other conservative Democrats. Plus, they didn't trust me.

When the DOT emerged from their closed session, Mrs. Randolph announced that although they might have supported Dollars for Democrats, they vowed "Not a Nickel for Pickle!" They declined to participate.

I always suspected DOT member and Yarborough associate Alex Dickie of coining the phrase. But regardless of who thought it up, it was catchy enough to make newspapers around the state. Eventually, Sam Wood, the editor of the *Austin American-Statesman* wrote a column critical of the DOT which ran in half a dozen newspapers across Texas. Wood's column earned him the DOT's wrath and his own nickname: "Switchblade Sam."

As word spread about "Not a Nickel for Pickle," wits all over Texas began mailing me letters. Inevitably, inside each envelope was a nickel and a note which went something like this: "Jake, I heard you needed a nickel, and so here is one. There just can't be too many nickels for Pickle!"

I had set up an old red card table and a file cabinet in my bedroom. When I wasn't at the SDEC, the card table served as my home office. As I opened the envelopes, I plunked the nickels in a pile, and finally gave them to ten-year-old Peggy. She remembers my great controversy fondly, because the nickels kept her in comic books and ice cream bars for weeks.

As far as I'm concerned, in terms of acrimony the worst state Democratic convention was the one held in San Antonio in 1958. In San Antonio, Department of Public Safety officers, guns on hips, strolled the convention floor as an incentive for order. Still, when the votes were cast and the liberals lost, delegates swarmed into the convention hall orchestra pit and attempted to climb on stage. As hatchet man, it fell to me to stand on stage and discourage people from breaching the ramparts! One stormer was former state senator Joe Hill from East Texas.

Hill was short, portly, and had high blood pressure. There he was, huffing and puffing, his face pink as ham, trying to heave himself out of the orchestra pit onto the stage—and me. I didn't want to shove him off, or get in a fist fight. The only thing I could think to do was step on his fingers! As I scraped his fingers off the stage with my shoe I said politely, "Sorry, Senator."

I consider myself a decent fellow, and although I don't think you could say I got ahead by stepping on people's toes, it *would* be accurate to say that in one instance I got ahead by stepping on people's fingers. Poor Joe Hill's, anyway.

During the commotion, most SDEC officials on stage beat a hasty retreat out the back door of the convention hall and headed for the Gunter Hotel. The DPS officers, a few skittish SDEC staffers, and I were left behind to hold the fort. Literally.

U.S. Congressman Frank Ikard, who at SDEC request had agreed to serve as temporary convention chairman, was taking it all in. Weeks before, in order to convince him to serve, I had told Ikard this was his chance to lend national authority to our peaceful expression of state democracy. Ikard's comment was, "Pickle, I sure do appreciate your inviting me to this *peaceful* convention!"

As I remember, liberal Democrat Maury Maverick, former mayor of San Antonio, finally led a bunch of angry delegates out of the convention hall and down the street to the Alamo, where they milled around in protest. But in the end, there was nothing they could do. We had the votes, and they didn't. It was raw and brutal politics.

The Dollars for Democrats campaign wasn't all that successful, but in a funny way, "Not a Nickel for Pickle" was. It brought me more publicity than any other phrase with which I was associated throughout my political career. Even years later, after I was elected to Congress, after lunch in the House of Representatives dining room, I would go to pay my bill and somebody would crack, "Hey, anybody got a nickel for Pickle?"

Also, the controversy brought me an off-hand compliment from a neighbor who misunderstood when she heard I was "a hatchet man." The neighbor said, "Why, Jake's a nice-looking man. He doesn't have a hatchet face at all!"

Nine

Steamboats up the Colorado

When the federal government began to build a series of dams above Austin in the 1930s and 1940s, Central Texas was transformed from dry caliche desert into a recreational paradise. In addition, dams stopped the devastating floods which had plagued Austin for hundreds of years. One of the biggest proponents of dam construction was Congressman, later Senator, Lyndon Johnson.

As dams were completed and more lakes added to Central Texas, people were agog. Creating all that available water was a project that stirred the popular imagination. Johnson himself was so impressed that he began to make extravagant predictions and claims about the possibilities of the lakes.

I was with the Senator one Saturday afternoon in Marble Falls, Texas, in the late 1940s. Gus Michel, Marble Falls' mayor, had blocked off Main Street and brought in a flatbed truck so Johnson could stand on it and speak. Johnson began talking about the beauties of the Highland Lakes. Then Johnson made this bold statement: "We're not finished yet. I will never rest until I see steamboats cruise up the Colorado and dock at the foot of the Congress Avenue bridge!"

The audience gasped and applauded. E. Babe Smith, LBJ's longtime friend standing in the audience, turned to me and said, "Jake, how can Lyndon do that?" And I said to Babe, "Damned if I know. Sounds like the craziest idea I ever heard!" Well, Babe thought that was so funny that later he made the mistake of repeating my comment to Johnson. In short order, Johnson called me to his office. He was boiling mad.

"I hear you've been making fun of my idea about steamboats up the Colorado," he fumed. "This is no joking matter! This is the thing of the future! Now, I don't want to hear any more talk about your ridiculing my steamboats."

"Yessir, yessir," I assured him. "From now on I'll be a *strong* advocate of steamboats." And I was.

Some twenty years later, when Johnson was President of the United States and I was the Tenth Congressional District's Congressman, I was feeling cocky and decided to tweak the President.

One day I told George Christian, Johnson's press secretary, "George, tell the President I'm going to introduce a bill in Congress next week to build a series of locks and dams from Galveston up to Austin. So that steamboats can cruise up the Colorado and dock at the foot of the Congress Avenue bridge. It won't cost but $2 billion."

A couple of weeks later I asked George if he had passed along my message to the President, and George said, "Yeah, I did."

"Well, what did he say?" I asked.

"He said, 'Tell Pickle that's the craziest idea I ever heard.'"

Today, every time I cross the Congress Avenue bridge, I look down, just in case any steamboats have made it up the river.

Bob Keckler's Cow

One of the nicest men I ever knew was Drew Gillen, a well-to-do cotton farmer from Blooming Grove, Texas. Drew was a prominent Democrat, highly respected, and a leader in his hometown Baptist congregation.

At the time—this was the early 1950s—I was acting as scheduler for Senator Johnson and, as such, traveled around the state with him. One of my responsibilities was selecting the times and places for the Senator to appear.

Drew kept insisting that Senator Johnson come to Blooming Grove to attend Drew's Baptist Men's Fellowship Class. It was, he assured me, a large and important group of Navarro County citizens.

After repeated requests, I recommended to Johnson that he accept Drew's offer and, somewhat reluctantly, he agreed. Johnson wasn't an avid churchgoer, and I think he had an aversion to mixing politics with religion.

But out of respect for Drew, Johnson finally agreed. When we arrived in Blooming Grove one afternoon in late fall, I discovered that the Fellowship Class met in an outdoor, octagon-shaped tabernacle which had no windows. The building's only ventilation was achieved by hoisting the walls up with pulleys and tying them in place. That night, while Johnson was speaking, a Texas blue norther blew in. We made the best of it we could, but the wind shook the tabernacle and swept through the raised walls. By the time Johnson finished speaking and the congregation finished praying, we were chilled to the bone. The men in our party—Johnson, Cliff Carter, Warren Woodward, and I—prayed mostly for heat.

Our next scheduled appearance was in Corsicana the next morning. As we walked out of the tabernacle, Johnson said, "Let's head for Corsicana quick!" It fell to me to admit to him, "Senator, I haven't made reservations in Corsicana, and besides, Drew insists we stay at his house."

Johnson exploded. After appearances he liked to chew the fat and plot strategy. He said, "Pickle, you know I don't like to stay in a private home. You KNOW I'd rather go to a hotel."

"Yes sir, I know that," I said, "but Drew insisted. He says he and Mrs. Gillen have made plans to stay with friends, so we'll have his place all to ourselves."

Johnson grumbled, but agreed to drive to Drew's home.

Often as we made swings around the state, reporters tried to get answers from Johnson about a current issue. They would catch him in person or ambush him by phone, day or night. One of Johnson's biggest antagonists was Clayton Hickerson with the Associated Press. Maybe because Hickerson was so persistent, Johnson never wanted to talk to him. Hickerson dogged us from town to town.

Somehow, Hickerson had found out where we were that night, and he kept calling us from Dallas. It was obvious he'd had enough to drink that he didn't give a damn how mad he made Johnson. The phone kept ringing and it would be Hickerson, asking for Johnson. We would answer the phone and call, "Senator, Clayton Hickerson's on the line," and Johnson would yell, "You tell that sonofabitch I'm not here!" We'd uncover the mouthpiece and tell Hickerson the Senator wasn't available.

We got ready for bed and turned off the lights. The phone kept ringing, and we let it ring. Hickerson called until after midnight.

Just when things got quiet, a cow outside our window began to bawl. It was a loud and mournful sound. No one could sleep. Hours passed with us lying in the dark, listening. Finally Johnson bellowed, "Do something about that cow!" So in the middle of the night I called Drew where he was staying across town. Woke everybody over there up. Drew drawled, "Oh, that's Bob Keckler's cow. They took her calf off 'er this morning, and she's callin' for it." Then he added inanely, "You know, I *told* 'em they ought not to do that."

I told Drew, "The Senator says you have to do something about that cow," so Drew got up and somehow, somewhere, found the calf and reunited it with its mother. As soon as the cow got her calf back, the incessant mooing stopped.

But by that time it was almost morning. We had to hit the road. Woodward, Carter, and I got dressed, but Johnson refused to get out of bed. He was tired and he was chilled. He hadn't slept a wink. He felt sure he was coming down with a cold. He kept saying, "You boys are trying to kill me!"

We stood over him and said, "Senator, we've got to be in Corsicana for breakfast. We got to go."

Johnson looked up at Warren Woodward. Then Johnson said, "Woody! Get down in this bed with me. What I need is some body warmth!"

Woody looked at Johnson. He looked at us. Then Johnson issued the order again. So, fully dressed, Woody lay down alongside Johnson— and under our watchful eyes.

As the Senator snuggled up to his bed partner, Woody, with big banjo eyes, looked up at me and said, "Pickle, you SOB, if you ever tell this, I'll kill you."

PART THREE

THE
WASHINGTON
YEARS

*The start of a thirty-one-year adventure: Beryl
and Jake leaving Austin for Washington,
D.C., and Jake's swearing-in ceremony,
December 23, 1963.*

Eleven

My First
Twenty-four Hours
in Congress

Throughout the 1950s and early 1960s, I remained active in politics, although as a campaign strategist, not a candidate. I had an appetite for politics. Even when it wore me out, it never bored me.

These years were personally wrenching for me. In 1952, after an illness of three years, Sugar died of breast cancer. Her death left me with a great sadness and a six-year-old daughter. Working long hours helped fill the void. I continued managing political campaigns and serving as Executive Director of the State Democratic Executive Committee.

In 1960 I married Beryl Bolton McCarroll, a widow with two sons, Dick and Graham. My family of two became a family of five, including three kids nearing college age. Fortuitously, Governor Price Daniel had just appointed me to the three-member Texas Employment Commission, and for the first time in decades, I had a steady paycheck—one that didn't depend on the vagaries of campaign victories. Money was tight, but while we weren't flush, we were doing OK.

But I hadn't gotten politics—campaign politics—out of my system. In 1963, my good friend Congressman Homer Thornberry, who represented Texas' Tenth Congressional District, announced his resignation from Congress to accept a federal judgeship. The vacancy left by Thornberry was too tantalizing for me to pass up. After so many years in politics, I *knew* the Tenth Congressional District. I had driven it a hundred times, and I was on a first-name basis with many of its Democratic Party leaders. In the spring of 1963, Lyndon Johnson was Vice President of the United States. I felt I could count on his support in my campaign.

From the time I announced for Congress in September 1963 to when I was elected in November, I campaigned so hard and covered so much territory (in 1963, Texas' Tenth Congressional District was ten counties wide) that I lost forty pounds. But I don't think even the rigors of that campaign prepared me for the whirlwind first twenty-four hours after I was sworn in.

After the election—and President Kennedy's assassination—then-President Johnson urged me to fly to Washington in late December, before the end of the first session of the 88th Congress. That way I could be sworn in a few days early. Johnson saw it as a great opportunity: if I were sworn in before other newly elected members of Congress (who couldn't be sworn in until mid-January), I would have a few days' seniority, an important consideration later when committee assignments were handed out.

So on December 23 Beryl and I flew Braniff Airlines to Washington, D.C. Dick, Peggy, and Graham stayed in Austin because we couldn't afford three additional airfares. When Beryl and I landed at National Airport, there was six inches of snow on the ground. Coming from sunny Texas, we thought that was pretty exotic. After a few years of snow, the novelty wore off, but that first Christmas, it seemed as if we had landed in a winter wonderland.

In advance of our arrival, Warren Woodward on LBJ's staff had invited us to stay overnight with him, and I had accepted. But waiting for us at National Airport was a long White House limousine. The driver tipped his hat and said politely, "The President and Mrs. Johnson send their regards, and invite you to spend tonight with them at the White House." This was the invitation of a lifetime, but I had been raised in West Texas, and taught that if you accepted one invitation, you couldn't cancel it for another.

So I told the driver, "Thank you very much, but we've already accepted an invitation from Mr. Woodward." When no one was looking, Beryl kicked me so hard on the shin she almost knocked me over. She said, "You nut! You aren't supposed to refuse an invitation to the WHITE HOUSE!" But I had already declined, so Beryl and I spent the night with Warren and his wife in Bethesda.

At 7:30 the next morning, Christmas Eve, 1963, I was sworn in as United States Representative. Actually, my credentials hadn't been officially received by the Clerk of the House of Representatives. But Rep. Charles Halleck, the House Republican leader, concurred with a request by Rep. Wright Patman, dean of the Texas delegation, and moved that I be sworn in anyway—"in the spirit of Christmas!"

Thirty minutes later, the House voted on the sale of wheat to Russia. President Johnson let it be known that he had kept Congress in session so late because he intended to pass this bill—or there would be no Christmas recess. He was subtle like that.

Now, throughout my campaign, I had preached a conservative approach to international affairs, saying I was tired of other nations getting our money, then turning around and kicking us in the shins. But that morning I voted aye, because $60 million dollars in gold, cash on the barrel head, sounded like a good deal to me, and it still does. The bill passed by six votes.

Shortly after the vote, I received a phone call from the White House, asking if Mrs. Pickle and I would like a ride back to Austin on Air Force One, which was leaving within the hour. This time I had the sense to accept. But first, I wanted a picture taken with Speaker of the House John McCormack. McCormack was finishing some business, which took a few minutes, and all the time Warren Woodward was tugging at my sleeve saying, "Hurry up, Jake. You can't keep the President waiting."

Finally, Beryl and I rushed out the north portico of the Capitol, where Warren had a car waiting. Because his own car was in the shop, he had been given a "loaner," which happened to be a Volkswagen bug. So the three of us squeezed into the Volkswagen, and Warren headed for the White House. We putt-putted down majestic Pennsylvania Avenue, the sides of which were piled with snow. Washington in the winter is a city of black and white contrast, marble and snow laced by tree branches. It can be austerely beautiful, and it was beautiful that day—our first.

When we got to the White House, a group of people were boarding two helicopters on the south lawn to fly to Andrews Air Force Base, departure site for Air Force One. Somehow, in the crush, Beryl and I got on the wrong helicopter. When we looked around, we realized that, along with several Presidential aides, we were in the press helicopter. Jack Valenti, who was seated beside us, grinned and said, "Jake, you're the only person in the world who'd make the President wait!" Because of this and because I knew Johnson wasn't keen about freshman Congressmen shooting their mouths off to the press, throughout the ride I feigned interest in the wintry countryside below.

At Andrews Air Force Base, another aide waved Beryl and me toward Air Force One, and we boarded, thinking it was the flight to Austin. Once airborne, we discovered we were part of an official delegation heading for Philadelphia to attend the funeral of Representative Bill Green, a man whom at that time I had never heard of nor met. Later, I learned that Bill Green was one of "the four Horsemen of the Congress," a handful of big city Congressmen who for many years maintained a powerful grip over Democratic votes. President Johnson, a close friend, was paying his respects.

I crept down the aisle of Air Force One, trying to determine when, if ever, the plane might land in Austin. When Johnson heard we were on board, he kidded me, then said with a smile, "We'll get to Austin later. But Jake, do you mind if we go to Philadelphia first?"

I stared at him in stupefaction. I could not comprehend myself nor anyone else on the planet saying to Johnson, "No, Mr. President, turn this plane around immediately and take us to Austin!"

When we landed in the City of Brotherly Love, it seemed like half the police cars in Philadelphia joined our caravan of limousines. With sirens screaming and lights flashing, we sped down the turnpikes in subfreezing temperatures. I was wearing a lightweight overcoat, perfect for Texas, but no more protection against the cold than if I had been wearing my bathrobe. Beryl had on a bright turquoise coat and white hat, bought in Austin for the festive occasion of my swearing in. Hardly somber funeral attire.

At the cathedral, where we wished to be inconspicuous, ushers directed us to a front pew. Throughout the ceremony, the tall cathedral doors were opened and shut as mourners passed through. As the icy wind blew in, Beryl and I huddled in our coats and tried to stay warm. I hoped people took our shivers as an expression of grief, rather than overexposure. When people introduced themselves, I looked grave and said we were friends of the family.

After the service, we were whisked via motorcade back to Air Force One, and this time we headed for Texas. When we landed at Bergstrom Air Force Base in Austin, the President said, "Let's go see John and Nellie." Governor Connally was still recuperating from wounds he had received on November 22. So the Secret Service drove the President, Lady Bird, Beryl, and me to the Governor's Mansion.

The Mansion, filled with friends, looked and smelled like Christmas. The Governor, his arm in a sling, stood beside Nellie greeting guests. But in a few minutes Beryl whispered to me, "Jake, we've got to go!" We needed to do some last-minute shopping; Christmas was just hours away. Outside the Mansion, a crowd had gathered, hoping for a glimpse of the President. When we slipped out the back door, people pressed up against the fence spotted us and, perhaps thinking we were LBJ and Lady Bird, cheered and applauded. Beryl and I waved back.

A kind soul—I don't remember who—drove us eight blocks to 6th and Congress, to E. M. Scarbrough & Sons, which was about to close. By that time, word had traveled over the wire services that Congress had approved the sale of wheat to Russia. And sure enough, one of my conservative friends and supporters, Austin businessman Noble Prentice, happened to be in Scarbrough's. He stopped me in the aisle and asked bluntly, "Jake, how'd you vote on the sale of wheat?"

It was my first accounting to a constituent. I took the offensive.

I said, "Now, Noble, during the campaign I told people that when they voted for me they weren't sending just *any* freshman to Congress. I know Washington. I know the President. I promised people that I'd be effective immediately.

"Now think about this," I added. "Congress has been laboring over the issue of foreign trade for six months, and has been completely deadlocked. I got to Congress and within thirty minutes, we passed a major bill. Now, how much more effective can you be?"

With that I turned and headed down the aisle. Noble called out,

"Wait just a minute—" but I kept going. Over my shoulder I called back cheerfully, "Merry Christmas, Noble!"

Beryl and I rushed up and down the aisles of Scarbrough's grabbing things—"We'll take this," "We'll take that." There was no time to debate. Everything was purchased within minutes.

When we got home, I took Graham and Peggy with me to buy a Christmas tree, and Beryl started wrapping presents. Somehow we got the tree up and decorated, with boxes under it.

The next morning—Christmas 1963—when we gathered our family around the tree, I thought, as I have thought every Christmas morning of my life, what a joy it is to be home at Christmas, surrounded by the people you love.

Twelve

The Closer
You Get

Early one morning in January 1964, not long after I arrived in Washington to begin my first term in Congress, I was invited to breakfast by my old U.T. classmate Frank Ikard. Ikard was an old Washington hand. He had served many years as U.S. Representative from Wichita Falls, and was in 1964—and for many years after—president of the American Petroleum Institute, one of the most powerful lobbies in Washington.

Ikard wanted me to meet some of his Congressional colleagues, especially members of the influential Ways and Means Committee. Mixing in that crowd was high cotton for a freshman Congressman because Ways and Means made committee assignments that could make or break your career. Not only that, Ikard offered to pick me up at the Washington Hotel, where I was staying, and drive me to the breakfast himself.

I settled back in the passenger's seat as Ikard drove up Independence Avenue toward the Capitol. It was a gray, misty day. A light rain was falling, which made visibility poor. We passed famous Washington landmarks in the fog, and Ikard did his best to be tour guide. He pointed out the old Forrestal Building, the beautiful Bartholdi fountain, and the "temporary" Navy offices erected during World War II.

As we approached the Capitol, on the right side of the car a gray shape loomed out of the fog. Frank said, "Jake, what do you think of that building?" I peered through the windshield. It was difficult to make out much of anything, except that the building was under construction. All I could see was a huge white rectangle streaked with calcium and covered with scaffolding. It seemed to stretch for blocks, as featureless and impersonal as a mausoleum.

I wasn't impressed, and responded with my immediate, honest reaction. I said, "Frank, that building looks kinda ugly to me."

"Well, I'm sorry to hear that," Ikard responded. "And I suggest you look again. I don't think Homer Thornberry would have said that."

"Why not?" I asked.

"Because if you look closely, you'll notice that the lower walls are faced with granite from Marble Falls, Texas—in *your* District. The building's named after the late Speaker of the House Sam Rayburn; I don't need to tell you what state *he* was from. The Sam Rayburn Office Building is the largest structure on Capitol Hill. It's a great tribute to Rayburn and Texas that this building is named in his honor."

I peered through the windshield as the wipers swooshed back and forth, and thought it over.

"You know, Frank," I said, "the closer you get, the better it looks!"

Thirteen

The Civil Rights Act

Of all my votes in Congress, I think my vote for the 1964 Civil Rights Act is the one of which I'm most proud.

As the new 88th Congress got underway in January 1964, it was obvious that President Johnson intended to pass significant humanitarian legislation. I don't know whether he had already formed the Great Society in his mind, but he definitely had an agenda and was anxious to get moving. One of the first items on that agenda was the Civil Rights Bill of 1964.

As early as 1958, Congress had flirted with civil rights by passing legislation which espoused equality in *principle*, but lacked the teeth to enforce it. But no Congress had attempted to pass an accommodations bill which insured basic privileges to people of all races.

Even in 1964, a century after the Civil War, some groups, especially blacks, didn't enjoy the basic rights we take for granted today, like staying in hotels, using public rest rooms, and patronizing many restaurants. This was especially true in the South, which championed states' sovereignty. It was argued that proprietors of businesses and local municipalities were the best judge of customers, and the federal government ought not to interfere.

After President Kennedy's assassination in 1963, Johnson had prom-

ised civil rights leaders he would move on this issue, and he was determined to do so. Essentially, Johnson was pushing a civil rights bill that
had been advanced in 1962 by Kennedy, but had gotten nowhere. Now
President Johnson put his full support behind the bill. He met with the
NAACP and the Civil Rights League, planning strategy.

Hostile Southern leaders threatened opposition, much as they had
done in the 1950s when they rallied behind the Southern Manifesto,
which championed the rights of proprietors over customers.

The Civil Rights Bill, sponsored by Rep. Emanuel Celler of New
York, Chairman of the House Judiciary Committee, was submitted to
the House of Representatives for action in early February 1964. The bill
had the strong support of the Judiciary Committee's minority leader,
Bill McCulloch—a Republican—as well. It was debated all week.

During my first Congressional campaign in 1963, civil rights was a
hot issue, but I never took a firm position. However, I left the impression that perhaps states should make these decisions. My friend Frank
Erwin, chairman of the University of Texas Board of Regents, who was
helping me garner votes, arranged with prominent East Austin busi-
nessmen O. H. Elliott and M. J. Anderson for us to meet with a group
of black ministers and community leaders to discuss the bill. Erwin
thought I would promise to support a civil rights bill, but I never made
that promise. I did say, "I'll read the bill and be open-minded." To be
honest, I still wasn't sure how I was going to vote.

Erwin blew a fuse. He said, "Damn you, Pickle! You had the chance
to get every black and brown vote in this district, and you didn't take it!"
He was disgusted with me.

As debate in the House started, Republicans and Democrats on the
Judiciary Committee clamored for permission to speak for or against
the bill. Soon, the time allotted for debate was taken. Amendment after
amendment was offered, and defeated. So sought after was the privilege
of addressing the House that no new member, in fact, hardly anyone
not on the powerful Judiciary Committee, was allowed to speak.

Each night, I took the bill back to my tiny efficiency at the Coronet
Apartments on Capitol Hill and read it over. That's always a mistake!
When you understand a bill thoroughly, it's harder to reject it outright.

But Beryl was in Texas with the kids, so each night I pored over the bill. I began to realize it wasn't anticonstitutional or punitive to states at all. It simply said that we shouldn't discriminate among races. I couldn't argue with that.

However, I decided to offer two amendments which I thought would make the bill more acceptable. I never had a chance. Debate had gone on so long, I couldn't get recognized. I offered both amendments "in block," meaning together. When I asked to have them separated for vote, permission was denied. I was so green I didn't know it wasn't acceptable to offer amendments in block, then vote on them separately.

I'll always remember the kindness of Mississippi Congressman Bill Colmer, a senior member of the House Rules Committee—and an opponent of the bill—who rose and said, "Mr. Speaker, the gentleman from Texas is offering an important amendment. This is his first amendment. I believe he is a promising new member of the House. In view of the fact that no debate has been allowed new members, I ask for unanimous consent that the gentleman be allowed to present his amendment, and that we vote on each separately."

No one wanted to be unfair, so I was allowed to offer my first amendment, which was promptly voted down by voice vote. Then I offered my second amendment—and it was voted down, too. The whole thing didn't take more than two minutes.

Dejected, I left the well at the front of the House and walked to the rear of the chamber. Bill Colmer called me aside, put his arm over my shoulders and drawled, "Now Jake, I know you're disappointed, but you mus' not take this purrrsonally. The members aren't in a mood to take amendments. I want you to look around this chamber. You don't know many of these people, but it doesn't matter from whence you come or whence you go, you'll find that these members will become your best friends in all the world. Take a good look. And remember that these members are just more interested in what happens in *their* district than in yours."

It was good advice, and I never forgot it.

Finally the vote was taken. As the roll call began, I still wasn't sure how I would vote. But I knew the bill wasn't the terrible miscarriage of justice that many Southerners claimed. So I voted for it. I was one of only six Southerners to do so. The others were Claude Pepper of

Florida, Charles Weltner of Georgia, and fellow Texans Albert Thomas, Henry B. Gonzalez, and Jack Brooks.

When the bill passed, there was a spattering of applause from supporters and angry denunciations from opponents. Most members—and I was one—wanted nothing more than to get out of there.

I agreed to meet Texas colleagues Olin Teague, Bob Casey, and Omar Burleson for dinner at the Rotunda, a favorite Capitol Hill watering hole and restaurant. Driving to the restaurant, I got lost and had to stop several times to ask directions. A cold misting rain turned into sleet. The weather seemed to match my somber mood.

The four of us stayed late at the Rotunda, drinking and talking. The consequences of the vote I had just cast weighed heavily on my mind. Had I sabotaged my Congressional career just as it was beginning?

By the time I got back to the Coronet it was nearly 2 A.M. As I walked through the lobby, the lady who ran the night switchboard, called out to me, "Congressman! The President has been calling. He wants you to call the White House."

I thanked her and said, "Well, it's too late now. I'll call him first thing tomorrow morning."

But she said, "Oh no, that's exactly what the President said you'd say. And he told me for you to be sure and call him tonight. If you don't call him, he'll just call back, and he's already called three times. Please, Congressman," she pleaded, terrified by the prospect of another conversation with Johnson, "call him now."

So I agreed. I went up to my room and placed a call to the White House operator. I told her, "Just leave word that I returned the President's call, and I'll call again first thing in the morning."

The White House operator said, "No, no, Congressman! Hold on. The President has been waiting for your call."

In a few seconds Johnson was on the line. He said, "Jake, it's pretty late." "Yessir, it is," I said.

"But I know where you've been," the President continued. "You've been out with friends having a few drinks, trying to forget that vote you made tonight. Isn't that right?"

I had to admit that was true.

"Well, it was a hard vote," the President continued. "But you know, I remember when I was in the House and Senate, I had the chance to vote for a bill like this one, and I never could quite bring myself to do it. But you did, Jake. So I said to myself that I wasn't going to let this night pass without telling you personally that your President is proud of you."

My throat closed up. I mumbled something inadequate like, "Yes sir, thank you, Mr. President," and hung up.

That bill became law. And though many people in my district were strong in opposition, I weathered the storm and was re-elected the following year. I've often wondered if I would have weathered the storm if I had been an incumbent with a track record, or if the President hadn't been my own constituent.

Even today, it's hard to believe that just thirty years ago people of color couldn't patronize many of the restaurants, hotels, public rest rooms, or water fountains in America. In retrospect, it's almost inconceivable that those conditions existed just a generation ago.

I believe that in 1964 a strong Civil Rights Bill could have passed only under the leadership of Lyndon Johnson. Nobody else knew how to manipulate Congress so effectively, or hammer through legislation by sheer force of will. And because Johnson was from Texas, he could look fellow Southerners in the eye and say, "I know what it will take for you to support this." He understood the risk.

A week after the vote, I was visiting with President Johnson and Jack Valenti at the White House. Jack commented that he was glad to see me vote for the bill. I told Valenti it was a hard vote, and then added with feeling, "I'm sure glad to get that one over with!"

President Johnson was listening and he said, "Jake, that *was* a tough vote. But you'll be in Congress for another twenty years (I surprised everybody—it was thirty-one years!) "and you'll probably have a civil rights vote every year from now on. We've just started civil rights reform, and we're two hundred years behind. We got a long way to catch up. So don't think for a second you've got this vote behind you!"

As usual, President Johnson was right.

And the fight continues.

*Three great characters: Jake, Culp Krueger—
and, at far right, the tail fins of the
White Shark.*

The White Shark

After I was elected to Congress, a lot of my friends from Austin suddenly decided it was time to visit Washington, and of course they wanted a tour of the Capitol and the White House—and most of all, a visit with "Lyndon." One of the first to insist was one of LBJ's early administrative assistants, my good friend Sherman Birdwell, who had succeeded me as a Texas Employment Commissioner.

I tried to tell Sherman tactfully that it might not be possible to see the President, and suggested as an alternative that I take him out to dinner at a fine Washington restaurant. That didn't suit Birdwell. He had his heart set on a personal visit to the White House, and although I kept discouraging him, Sherman wouldn't take no for an answer.

So I called Lady Bird, who knew and liked Sherman, and secretly arranged for us to drop by the next evening. But I said nothing of these plans to Sherman.

At the time I was driving a 1959 white Chrysler New Yorker, a car distinguished by enormous tail fins and a space-age bubble dashboard lit with turquoise lights. It became well known on Capitol Hill for its dramatic lines, especially the fins, which could be spotted several blocks before the rest of the car. My staff affectionately referred to the Chrysler as "the White Shark."

As we drove around Washington that day, Sherman said he was

disappointed he wasn't going to get to see Lady Bird and Lyndon, and I told him "Look, you can't just drive up to the White House and say, 'I'm here to see the President.'" "Oh Hell," Birdwell said, "face it, Pickle. You just don't have enough stroke to get us in."

In a few minutes I wheeled up to the South Gate of the White House. The guard, who, unbeknownst to Birdwell, had been told to expect me, said, "Oh hello, Congressman Pickle. How are you this evening?" I told the guard, "We'd like to see the President," and the guard said, "Well, of course, Congressman. You're *always* welcome."

Birdwell looked at me with new respect. "Gol-ley, this is something," he said as we were waved through the gate.

We parked the Chrysler in the wide circular driveway beneath the Truman Balcony and were ushered into the family dining room, where the Johnsons were having dinner. Birdwell was still in the dark about how I had set it up.

The President and Lady Bird greeted us warmly, and the President, who was a natural raconteur, settled in a chair and started telling stories. I was relishing friends in high places and Birdwell was having the time of his life, when Lee, the White House maitre d', entered the room briskly and came to stand beside my chair. He asked in a clear, loud voice, "Congressman, do you have a white Chrysler?" "Why, yes," I said.

"Well, Congressman, your car is on fire," Lee said.

I jumped to my feet. Lee continued matter-of-factly, "Yes sir, it has caught fire, but the Secret Service think they have it under control."

I was starting out of the room when Johnson raised his hand, "Lee, is the car actually burning?" he asked.

"No sir, the Secret Service has poured water on the engine," Lee said.

And Johnson said, "Well then, sit down, Jake, and let me finish my story!" So upon Executive Order from the President of the United States, I slumped back in my chair.

When I was finally able to excuse myself, I rushed outside to discover that sure enough, the car's electric wiring had somehow ignited, causing the Chrysler to smolder and finally to burst into flames. When the fire was extinguished, the car was rendered stone cold dead weight— smack in front of the White House.

Chagrined, Sherman and I caught a ride home that night. I left the

Chrysler at the White House until the next day, when a member of the President's staff called and insisted I come down to "identify" my car for the wrecker service. I was so embarrassed I refused. I even tried to talk Beryl into claiming it, and *she* refused. Neither one of us wanted to be seen with the Chrysler in its disreputable condition. Finally, White House staffers had the car towed away on their own authority, and sent the bill to me.

Over the years, the Chrysler became famous in Washington for having a personality all its own, and for what some claimed was the cavalier way I attended to its service. People regarded it fondly, as though it were a recalcitrant but lovable relative. Often, people would pass me in the halls of Congress and call back over their shoulder, "Jake, how's the White Shark?"

It was a great car!

Being a witness to its catching fire at the White House wasn't Sherman's worst experience with the White Shark. Years later in Austin I left it in Sherman and Delle Birdwell's driveway, which sloped downhill to their garage. Either I didn't put the Chrysler in park or I didn't set the emergency brake, and the car began to roll, picking up momentum until it smashed right through the garage door. Sherman and I were in the back yard when we heard the crash. We ran around the corner to find the garage knocked off center, leaning crazily on its foundations, the fins of the white shark poking out of the splinters like feathers on an arrow.

And once I drove Austin humorist Cactus Pryor back to Washington from a Texas State Society picnic near Mount Vernon in Virginia. Halfway through the drive the White Shark's brakes gave out—apparently all the brake bands had worn away. When I applied the brakes, it was metal on metal, and we came to an abrupt and violent stop.

It took me over an hour to drive ten miles, with us jerking all the way and Cactus white-knuckled on the seat beside me. Ever since then, Cactus refers to that incident darkly as "one of the most harrowing experiences of my life!"

Incidentally, I owned the Chrysler until 1975, when reluctantly I sold it for $100—just about what I paid that morning to have it hauled away from the White House.

Pop and LBJ got along fine.
Pop admired Johnson's politics and the
President admired Pop's spunk.

Fifteen

Pop Goes to Washington

WASHINGTON (UPI)—FARMER, 88, GETS LBJ PLANE RIDE.
J. B. Pickle of Big Spring, Tex., took his first airplane ride
Monday at the age of 88. What's more, he rode with President
Johnson.

Pickle, father of Rep. J. J. Pickle, D-Tex., was invited aboard
Johnson's plane, Air Force One, on its return flight to Washington
from New York where the President made a major speech.

Johnson was so delighted to have the elder Pickle aboard that he
asked newsmen back to his lounge to meet him.

"Nowhere but in the United States could an ordinary clodhopper—I'm just a retired farmer and groceryman—be invited to ride
in the President's plane," Pickle told reporters.

Pickle's son, who is from Austin, numbers the President among
his constituents and also was aboard the plane.

During the 50-minute flight, Pickle appeared relaxed as he sat in
the window seat of a sofa, Johnson beside him. But he did confess:

"I don't feel secure. It's a long way down, from here to the
ground."

However, he said, he was willing to make the flight because "I've
lived 88 years, and I don't have much longer to live."

♦ ♦ ♦

This wire service article and others like it appeared in newspapers around the country in April 1964. Joseph Binford Pickle—whom our family called "Pop"—was a lot more than a clodhopper, although he was proud to call himself one, or anybody else that did an honest day's work. Although Pop farmed during his long life—*and* herded sheep, traded mules, and worked as an oil field roustabout to make a living—based on longevity of occupation, he was a retired newspaperman and grocer from West Texas. In the spring of 1964, Pop decided the recent election of his rapscallion son Jarrell was momentous enough to warrant a trip to Washington, D.C., a place he revered but had never seen. Mom, his wife of sixty years, had died after a long illness. Pop wanted to stay busy.

And although the article was right about his age, Pop was wrong about not having much longer to live. He lived to be just two months shy of his ninety-fifth birthday. But in many ways, that trip to Washington, which included his first helicopter and airplane rides, was a high point in his life. Pop's heroes were the Founding Fathers, Franklin Roosevelt, and Harry Truman, in that order. He was willing to add Lyndon Johnson to the list—as long as Johnson proved his mettle.

Uncharacteristically, I took a back seat in this drama. You'll notice that the above article refers to me as "Pickle's son," which about sums up Pop's visit. If, full of self-importance during my freshman year in Congress, I had envisioned grandly showing off "my Washington" to my eighty-eight-year-old father, somehow events flip-flopped, and I was tagging after *Pop*. But let me start at the beginning.

Pop got to Washington because of a felon, and it wasn't me! My brother-in-law, Miller Harris, was sheriff of Howard County, and he had to transport a prisoner to Texas. So Miller and a deputy drove Pop two thousand miles to Washington, D.C., dropped him off at my office, picked up the prisoner, handcuffed the man to the door handle, and went back to Texas. The long drive from Big Spring was OK with Pop, because he had never flown and was in no hurry to start.

The afternoon Pop arrived, the first thing I did was take him down to the Tidal Basin. Pop walked the length of the Basin, marveling at the cherry blossoms, which were in full bloom. He stood in the middle of the Jefferson Memorial, reciting from memory Jefferson's quotations chiseled in stone, and commenting on his progressive spirit. "Not," he told me and every tourist within earshot, "like those Republicans today."

The next morning he accompanied me to my office in the Cannon Office Building. My staff, especially George Bristol, fell in love with him and, while I was on the House floor, squired him around the Hill. When things got quiet, Pop wandered off by himself, down the hall to other Congressional offices. As introduction he would say, "My boy Jarrell's in Congress." Then he would ask his usual questions: "How's the weather and crops in your district?" "Think the Democrats will win in your state this fall?" And of course, people would have to stop working and chat with the elderly gentleman from Texas. Oh, Pop was well known on my floor!

That afternoon I took him on a tour of the Capitol. An enormous canvas depicting the Battle of Lake Erie hung in a stairwell on the Senate side, and before I could say a word, he quoted verbatim:

> The 10th of September, a date to remember
> As long as the world on its axis turns round
> The Tars and the Greens on Lake Erie were seen
> To bring the proud flag of Great Britain down . . .

I had passed that painting dozens of times and never thought a thing about it. Here was Pop, educating *me*. He said he had learned the poem in school eighty years before, and it "stuck in my mind." Pop was a voracious reader. He even read the dictionary and the *Encyclopedia Britannica*. When he finished volume Z, he started over again.

Speaker John McCormack spotted me and waved us into his private office. Immediately, Pop began peppering McCormack with ideas, such as taxing large chain stores. When Pop concluded with, "Don't you think so?" the Speaker turned pleading eyes on me. I quickly said, "Well, that's certainly something to think about . . . !" and maneuvered Pop toward the hall. After that, for as long as I knew John McCormack, he always inquired about Pop.

That night Warren Woodward hosted a party at his house in Potomac, Maryland, and he said to bring Pop along. So I did. Pop went about the room meeting people, sticking out one hand, and cupping his ear with the other, because he was hard of hearing. As he was introduced to the third or fourth person he fixed his eyes on the fellow's chest and strained to catch his name. It was "The President, Lyndon Johnson." Pop jerked backward, and his eyes traveled up the tall frame until they reached Johnson's face. "LYNDON JOHNSON!" he exclaimed. "Well, by jingo, imagine that!"

Johnson laughed heartily. He was used to people schmoozing and flattering him, so he enjoyed Pop's spontaneous reaction. The two men sat down and talked. Johnson asked Pop if he would like to come to the White House the next day and have his picture taken, and Pop agreed. Driving home, I teased Pop, "What do you think about that!" Pop replied candidly, "Well, it can't hurt him a bit!" meaning Johnson could not be unaware of the down-home publicity potential of being photographed with a retired farmer. But I could tell the old man was honored.

The next morning we visited the Folger Library. Pop looked at a bust of William Shakespeare and told me, "Look at that face. You can see how intelligent he was!" At the Lincoln Memorial, he was so moved, I thought he would cry. At Ford's Theater, I had to pull him away. That afternoon, when I took him to the National Archives, he bounded up the steps ahead of me, then stopped and asked if I needed help.

Inside, Pop couldn't make out the documents, which are encased behind thick glass, but when I read aloud a phrase from each, he would complete the sentence. I quit explaining history to him when I showed him the Northwest Ordinance. "Oh yes," Pop said right away. "That was in 1787, you remember, when the Union took in Ohio . . ."

Finally at the appointed hour we arrived at the White House and were ushered into an anteroom. As we sat there, suddenly the two large double doors of the room burst open and men came running through. Pop jumped to his feet, as startled as I, but the men ran past us. Pop thought it was a riot, but it was only the end of a Presidential press conference. The men were reporters, dashing for phones.

That day Pop had his picture taken with the President of the United States. I stood to one side and watched them. Then the three of us had lunch. Pop did most of the talking. He advised the President on a good many things! Together, the President of the United States and my eighty-eight-year-old father promised to take a razor strap to me if I got out of line on votes and forgot the common man.

Johnson enjoyed baiting Pop. He would say something like, "Well, I'd like to pass (such-and-such legislation), but those fellows in Congress"—he'd nod in my direction—"won't support me." "Oh, my goodness!" Pop would exclaim in alarm. "Jarrell! Is that right?" And Johnson would grin as I tried to wiggle off the hook. When Johnson asked Pop what he thought about Republicans, Pop said, "There's not but three or four of them that are any good." "Which ones?" Johnson asked, and quick as a flash Pop replied, "Javits, Cooper, Case, and Clark."

That afternoon Pop and I toured Mount Vernon, and that evening we went to a party at the Women's Democratic Club near Dupont Circle. When we arrived, Pop's reputation had preceded him. Everyone clustered around "Mr. Pickle." When someone teased Pop they had to watch his son closely, Pop said, "You don't have to tell me anything about Jarrell. I've known him all his life!" That line got the biggest laugh of the evening.

Then the miracle happened again. A phone call from the White House: the President wanted to visit with Pop again. Would he like to come back to the White House?

Would he! Soon a big black limousine arrived for us, and back we went. This time Lady Bird, the President, Pop, and I sat in the family's living quarters, talking politics as the Johnsons ate a late dinner. Pop commented on the world situation—why the United States should fight in Vietnam, how fortunate the country was to have Johnson as President after Kennedy's assassination, and why Republicans couldn't be trusted. Johnson couldn't get Pop to eat anything. Pop refused, saying it wasn't healthy to eat a big evening meal. Then he looked at the President's full plate and paunch, cleared his throat, and repeated this information. Lady Bird, who was always trying to get her husband to diet, nodded as she listened, saying, "I agree, I agree."

Then we went into the President's bedroom, where we went over the text to a speech that Johnson was scheduled to deliver Monday in New York City. Around 11 P.M. a limousine drove us back to the Coronet. It was the first time in years that Pop, who went to bed with the chickens and got up with the roosters, stayed awake past 9 P.M. In the limousine Pop mused aloud over the events of the day, saying, "Oh my goodness, just think of it! I wonder why, I wonder why."

I knew why. I suspect Pop reminded the President of his own father, crusty Sam Johnson. Despite his age, Pop was sharp as a tack. He understood the issues of the day, and their relation to history. He was the original yellow-dog Democrat. Pop's spunk amused Johnson. Also, Johnson enjoyed gigging me.

Although he had great respect for the presidency, Pop viewed Johnson and everybody else in government as public servants. In Pop's opinion, no elected official was above answering to the average citizen. Johnson, who knew instinctively who was afraid of him and how to capitalize on that fear, knew just as instinctively when he was confronted with the real thing. Pop was the real thing.

So I wasn't all that surprised the next day when the President called to invite us to fly with him to New York on Monday. I thanked Johnson, but said that I might have to decline, since the House would be in session that day. Also, I knew Pop hadn't flown before. I wanted to give him a graceful way out.

Back at my apartment at the Coronet, Pop contemplated this turn of events. He was torn, and we discussed it at length. I encouraged him to accompany the President without me, but he was reluctant. Finally Pop slammed both hands down on the arms of his chair, a gesture of finality I knew so well, and said, "Jarrell, in my opinion, we must *not* miss this opportunity!" So I decided that if Pop could risk an airplane ride, I could risk a day of missed votes. We accepted the President's invitation.

The next morning we flew in a helicopter from the White House to Andrews Air Force Base, where we boarded Air Force One. At thirty thousand feet, Pop ate a big steak in the President's dining room. The steak was followed by blackberry cobbler. When blackberry seeds got in Pop's teeth, he took out his dentures and cleaned them with his handkerchief—right in front of the Man.

After we landed, as our motorcade sped through New York, people lined the streets, waving and cheering at the President. Johnson kept telling Pop, "Wave at them, Mr. Pickle!" At the same time, Pop directed a steady barrage of questions—"What's that building? How many people live in New York City?"—at our official escort, Deputy Mayor Paul Scrivane. When Pop asked Scrivane where Mayor (Robert) Wagner was, Scrivane said he was tied up. Johnson added, "The mayor's a busy man, you know," and Pop said, "Yes, but the President of the United States is a busy man, too!"

When we arrived at the Waldorf-Astoria, half the photographers in New York were waiting. As we got out of the limousine, you could hear the buzz—"Who is he? Who is he?"—meaning Pop. The next morning, the *New York Times* carried a picture of Johnson and Pop entering the Waldorf-Astoria. The cutline read "President Lyndon Johnson and unidentified man . . ."

On the flight back to Washington, the President called in four newsmen traveling with us and introduced them to Pop. This was the interview that resulted in articles about Pop in newspapers across the country, including Pop's remark to reporter Bob Considine that he wasn't worried about the long way to the ground because he didn't have much longer to live anyway.

The interview went fine until Pop unintentionally turned the tables on Johnson by asking the reporters, "Don't you boys think the applause was a little weak today?" You can be sure the President quickly re-took control of *that* interview!

Back at Andrews Air Force Base, Johnson stepped up to the microphone and, after saying a few words, introduced Pop to the crowd. I held my breath and tried to hear what Pop was saying, but couldn't because of the roar of the engines. The President slapped me on the shoulder and said Pop did "Fine, just fine!" To this day, I don't know exactly what Pop said.

The next morning Pop braved his third airplane ride in eighty-eight years, this time a commercial flight back to Texas. It had been, he told me, a fairy-tale trip. "Oh my, Jarrell, just imagine!" he said. At Dulles Airport he hugged me tightly, and then he was gone. It was to be his only trip to Washington.

The afternoon of Pop's departure, the President called to inquire about Pop, and I told him he was gone—back to Big Spring and his memories. With enormous emotion, I thanked the President for the attention he had lavished on my father. Johnson said, "Listen, Jake, your old man knows what he's talking about. You can't fool him one minute. *And* he's got a heart. He's a rare jewel. You take good care of him; he's priceless." When the President of the United States brags on your father, I tell you it raises goose bumps on the back of your neck.

Pop talked about his trip to Washington for the rest of his life. He considered himself a sort of civilian advisor to the President of the United States. He saw his trip as an example of what the Declaration of Independence meant when it said ". . . governments are instituted among men, deriving their just powers from the consent of the governed." Whenever Pop went to the barbershop or the Baptist Men's Fellowship, he would relive the fabulous tale. He would begin, "My boy Jarrell's in Congress . . ."

Over the next few years I heard second hand that Johnson told people, using the graphic, barnyard language he employed so well, "Jake came from good stock. You can always tell a good product by the stud."

I was the product—but Pop was the stud!

And so ended the story of Pop's trip to Washington. But there was one last chapter. Six years later, in 1970, Pop died in Big Spring following a stroke. I was in Fort Worth when I got the news, and flew immediately to Big Spring. Family and friends gathered at the Nalle-Pickle funeral home, run by cousin J. C. Pickle. Just before the service started, in walked the President and Lady Bird. Johnson, who in 1968 had announced he would not run for re-election, had flown to Big Spring from the LBJ Ranch.

As they walked down the aisle and I rose to greet them, Johnson whispered in my ear, "Jake, you had a *good* daddy!"

In three years, the President was gone, as well.

My First
Embassy Party

Shortly after my election to Congress and arrival in Washington, D.C., Ambassador and Mrs. Dick Seppala of Finland invited me to attend a party at the Finnish Embassy. Theirs was my first embassy invitation. The Seppalas were friends of President and Mrs. Johnson, and I suspect I was invited as a courtesy to Lady Bird and LBJ.

Although I was flattered to be included, I didn't know a thing about "the embassy circuit"—the rounds of elegant parties to which members of Congress are invited. While I was trying to make up my mind whether to go, my administrative assistant, Bob Waldron, urged me to accept. Bob was a Washington insider: he had been Congressman Homer Thornberry's administrative assistant for several years before my election. Bob knew and appreciated social niceties, and he said it was important for a new Congressman to meet and mingle with the leaders of foreign countries and other dignitaries.

Another reason for my hesitation was that the party was a white-tie affair. I didn't know what to wear and I didn't know how to act. Cautiously, I admitted to Bob that I owned a tuxedo. "Oh no, Congressman," he said, horrified. "That would not be enough!" He said I had to have the full regalia, and rented me white tie and tails.

I thought I would just drive myself there, but Bob vetoed that, too. He said, "Congressman, you can't park blocks from the embassy and walk down the street in white tie. You must have a chauffeur. I'll drive you. And protocol says you must arrive *exactly* on time."

I didn't think a chauffeur was necessary, but Bob insisted. He even secured a chauffeur's cap and wore a dark suit, so that I could arrive in style, exactly on the appointed hour.

Which I did. At 6:30 P.M. sharp on a spring evening in 1964, I was deposited at the front door of the Finnish Embassy by my administrative assistant, wearing a serious expression and a duck-billed cap. As we came to a stop in front of the embassy, Waldron raced around to my side of the car—my own 1959 Chrysler New Yorker—where I sat in the back seat feeling ridiculous. With a flourish, Waldron opened the door and bowed slightly. In all my rented grandeur, I alighted and was admitted to the party.

Inside the embassy, I tried my best to make acquaintances. I didn't know a soul and not a soul knew me—or cared. Later, I discovered that embassy parties are somewhat clannish; people on the circuit recognize and socialize with each other. They don't know many people on the Hill, especially awkward new Congressmen.

After I had milled around a while by myself I became frustrated and about half angry. I wasn't recognized. I wasn't meeting anybody. I might as well have been a potted palm. All around me people were speaking Finnish, French, Italian, and German, but no one was speaking Texan.

Finally I decided to take charge of the situation. I would engage some of these prominent people in conversation. I scanned the crowd and picked out the most important looking, best-dressed man in the room. I walked up to him, squared my shoulders, stuck out my hand, and said, "I'm Jake Pickle from Austin, Texas. I'm the new Congressman from the Tenth Congressional District. I'm the President's Congressman. What's your name?"

"Good evening, sir," he said evenly. "I am Pierre. May I get you a drink?"

With that reply, sheepishly I faded into the shadows.

However, during the course of the party I did learn a few things about protocol. When dinner was seated, they served hors d'oeuvres and a salad. I thought it was the main course, and I ate every morsel of food on my plate, scraped it clean, and took a little extra to be polite. By the time they brought the fish course, I was so full, I couldn't eat a thing. I pushed the food on my plate around with my fork while my dinner companions chatted and toasted their way through a six-course meal.

During the first course, Congressman (and later Mayor of New York) John Lindsey, already a seasoned politician, arrived to take center stage. Apparently *he* wasn't bound by the time constraints of protocol! Lindsey, a handsome, urbane man, was a favorite on the circuit. All conversation was directed to Lindsey and none to me. I sat uncharacteristically silent and watched the proceedings like a spectator at the theater.

On the other hand, I departed like Cinderella at the appointed hour, when my chauffeur drove up in a car with the longest tail fins in Washington and retrieved me. Once settled in the back seat, I lied and told Bob, "Oh, it was a great party! I made a lot of friends. Especially Pierre."

Bob was delighted. He said, "Congressman, I knew you would."

The irrepressible Ed Clark, 1991.
Photo by Allen Searight, PIBC19497.
Courtesy of Austin History Center,
Austin Public Library.

Seventeen

Bless Their
Hearts

One of the most austere and somber parties I ever attended was in 1967
in the United States Supreme Court Building in Washington, D.C.

Associate Justice Tom Clark hosted a party to honor his lifelong
friend Ed Clark, who had been appointed by President Johnson as
Ambassador to Australia. Also attending the party was Sir Keith Waller,
Australia's Ambassador to the United States, and Lady Waller. Justice
Clark invited perhaps fifteen couples, including a smattering of Congressmen and members of the Supreme Court. Beryl and I felt very
privileged to be included.

Just how privileged became apparent when we arrived. It was a white-
tie affair! Ahead of time, I'd had to rent tails and even a pair of white
gloves. Upon arriving at the Supreme Court, we were ushered into a
huge reception room. Waiters in evening clothes tiptoed about serving
drinks and appetizers on silver trays. We sipped our drinks and gazed
at ancient portraits of former Supreme Court Justices, their solemn
countenances glowering down at us. As a fire blazed in the hearth, a
string ensemble played classical music. We spoke in low tones, awed by
our surroundings and the grand solemnity of the occasion.

Then we were ushered into the dining room, where more somber
portraits hung on the walls, and a formal dinner—presented on the left
and removed on the right—was served by waiters whose gloves were
even whiter than mine.

At the conclusion of the dinner, Justice Clark introduced Sir Waller. The Australian Ambassador, in his clipped Aussie accent, related how he and Lady Waller had learned to love "the Yellow Rose of Texas," as Australians called Ed Clark. In sincere and eloquent terms he said that Edward Clark was the most loved American ever to serve in Australia.

"On many occasions we have called on him for help, and we learned he had a direct line to the President of the United States," intoned Waller. "Australia will never forget his dedication, and the dedication of his lovely wife Ann."

Then Justice Clark called on Ambassador Clark. Ed rose and began to talk about his great love for Australia and the Australian people who, he said, "are more like Texans than Texans." Clark emphasized how Keith and Lady Waller had become like members of the Clarks' own family.

He concluded by calling Australia "the bastion of freedom of Southeast Asia and a true friend of every American."

As Clark spoke, absentmindedly he began to comb his hair with three fingers (he had lost two fingers in a lumber accident as a young man), closed his eyes, and reminisced in reverential terms about what Australia meant to him and Ann. When at last he opened his eyes, there were tears in them.

It was an emotional moment.

When Ambassador Clark finished, Justice Clark rose and said, "We've just enjoyed two wonderful toasts that have touched us all. But now I believe there is one more toast that should be given." Then he raised his glass and said, "I propose a toast to the ladies—bless their hearts."

Whereupon Ed Clark inexplicably burst out, "And all their other vital organs!"

There was a sudden hush; then Ann Clark turned to her husband and cried, "Edward! Ed-WARD!" At the same time, Lady Waller, who'd sucked in her midsection in an astonished gasp, released her breath with a whoosh that was heard halfway down the table.

But for the rest of us—our laughter became great waves that filled the room—the tension of that swellegant, elegant evening had been broken.

Eighteen

(Don't) Smoke, Smoke, Smoke That Cigarette

CAUTION: Cigarette smoking may be hazardous to your health.
—THE FIRST WARNING LABEL ON CIGARETTE PACKS,
1965

Once when we were kids in Lamesa, Joe, Janice, Jeanette, and I snuck off to the barn to smoke. Baby Judith was too young to be corrupted. Mostly, Joe and I were showing off for our giggling older sisters. We stripped cedar bark from fence posts, crumpled the bark into powder, and rolled it in paper to make crude cigarettes. Of course, we didn't enjoy the taste. We enjoyed the vision of ourselves smoking. Like men of the world.

But children playing with matches in dry barns are an even bigger health threat than cigarettes; sure enough, we accidentally started a small fire. Although we doused it quickly, Mom heard us hollering, rushed down to the barn, and discovered what we had been doing. When Pop came home, she met him at the door with the news. Pop was a teetotaling Baptist who didn't appreciate the attraction of sin. He set out to teach us a lesson.

Pop said, "By jingoes, you want to smoke, let's do it right!" He marched us four kids out to the front porch. He found a corncob pipe, filled it with cedar, and handed the pipe to us. Before, we had been puffing at our makeshift cigarettes, but not really drawing smoke into our lungs. Now Pop insisted we inhale. He stood over us while we took turns. After about the third puff, I was queasy. When the pipe was empty, Pop filled it again, saying, "You kids think you enjoy this, let's have another!" By the time he let us quit, we were sick as dogs. As I remember, I went around the corner of the house and vomited.

That took care of my desire to smoke for at least a decade.

But when I went off to the University of Texas, I started to smoke again. In the thirties, smoking was associated with the lives of sophistication and affluence we saw portrayed in movies. The same thing attracts kids today, but it was doubly attractive during the Depression. Smoking was the thing to do. Almost everybody did it, and nobody really thought it was harmful—at least I didn't.

I learned to drink beer at Fritz's Barn, a beer joint near campus, and I learned to smoke at Little Campus Dorm. We Little Campus boys rolled cigarettes in our rooms, using tobacco and paper bought at the drugstore and hand-rolling machines that cost about a dollar; most boys owned one. You produced this lumpy little cylinder that sagged in the middle and leaked tobacco onto your shirt, but it was cheap. Few of us could afford store-bought smokes.

We smoked pipes, too. A pipe was even more sophisticated than a cigarette. We were just a bunch of skinny, rail-thin boys, but we sat around our rooms chomping on pipe stems like Errol Flynn.

I wasn't hiding out in the barn anymore; I was a college man in the big city. I felt like a man of the world.

I continued smoking off and on for about twelve years, including the first year of my Naval service in the Pacific. Then I quit, because smoking, coffee, and the possibility that I might be blown to smithereens aggravated my stomach. After I came home from the war, I didn't start smoking again, although I liked a cigar once in a while. Sugar and a lot of our friends smoked, but that didn't tempt me. After I kicked the habit, I didn't want anything to do with cigarettes.

Over a decade later, after my election to the House of Representatives, I became a member of the House Interstate and Foreign Commerce Committee's subcommittee on health. My subcommittee was asked to address the issue of cigarette smoking. The questions we grappled with were (1) was smoking dangerous? and (2) what, if anything, should the government do about it?

You have to remember that thirty-five years ago, most Americans believed that although cigarette smoking might be harmful for *some* people, it wasn't a major health risk for the general population. Whenever public health researchers or epidemiologists accused the tobacco industry of manufacturing a hazardous product, the cigarette companies could—and did—claim there was no proof.

Then in 1964 the Surgeon General of the United States, Luther Terry, published a report that said cigarette smoking contributed to a variety of health problems, including increasing the risk of cancer. The report caused quite a stir, and my subcommittee on health was asked to look into it.

Opinion among the dozen or so members of our subcommittee was mixed. Some members favored economic sanctions, including eliminating subsidies to tobacco farmers, or even a ban on the sale of tobacco. Other members, like Horace Kornegay (D-N.C.) and Dave Satterfield (D-Va.) were from tobacco-producing states, and urged us to consider how agricultural communities that depended on tobacco would be devastated if we suddenly banned their livelihood.

Our chairman was the brilliant Paul Rogers (D-Fla.), and *he* thought something should be done. We argued the issue back and forth. How could we help the most people and hurt the fewest?

I took the position that one thing we *could* do was inform people what our nation's doctor had said—that cigarette smoking is hazardous to your health. Finally the subcommittee recommended legislation requiring a warning on each pack of cigarettes manufactured and sold in the United States—so that anyone who picked up a cigarette pack had to be aware of the risk. It was a compromise, but that's what legislation is about: compromise. I was a cosponsor of the bill.

The tobacco companies decided not to fight us when we passed the bill out of subcommittee to the full Commerce Committee. From the tobacco industry's standpoint, a cigarette pack warning was preferable to a ban. The legislation passed the House and Senate and became law in 1965.

Over the years, that original warning has been strengthened. Today, as for the past thirty-one years, every pack of cigarettes manufactured in the United States carries one of two stern warnings.

Critics say it isn't much. However, three decades ago it was a major step—one of the *first* steps—toward raising public consciousness about the risks associated with smoking.

Have warnings on cigarette packs caused people to quit smoking? I don't know. But I believe it has caused them to think. Most successful antismoking efforts in this country grew out of that courageous Surgeon General's report and the reaction it generated.

Seventy-five years ago, when Pop made us kids smoke that corncob pipe, he was issuing his own health warning: "Caution, Joe, Janice, Jeanette, and Jarrell: smoking will be hazardous to *your* health!"

Nineteen

Listening
for the Bell

During the Abscam scandals of the 1970s, sometimes it seemed to me that every night on the television news we would watch a new tape of a member of Congress or another government official accepting money for favors. The image was pretty much the same: a surveillance camera in a meeting room or hotel captured the grainy, gray and white image of people negotiating their price. When confronted with the evidence, the objects of the sting usually claimed they were trying to help a constituent, or just practicing a little law (or real estate, or consulting) on the side.

I watched these films with a feeling of dread and sorrow.

At the time, as today, there was a lot of controversy about the issue of entrapment. Is it fair to set up a situation that not only allows—but encourages—people to behave unethically? Do people being bribed always know it? Do political contributions always come with strings attached?

There is an even bigger issue at stake, and that is character. Character is one of those words that is thrown around a lot, especially during an election year. But what is "character" in a public official? Every person in public life faces these questions eventually. How you handle them affects your career and defines your ethics.

During Abscam my daughter asked me if things were always black and white. Was it possible to think you were helping a constituent when you were really being improperly influenced? "How hard is it to know when you cross the line?" she asked. "Are there times when you really DON'T know?"

I thought a minute, then said what I believe, which is "Nope. Deep down inside you know when somebody's asking for monkey business. You just have to listen for the bell."

I believe that most of us have a little internal bell, a kind of alarm that goes off when something isn't right. It's tucked away in a corner of your brain. When it goes off, it isn't loud, like a buzzer. It's a quiet bell. Often you have to strain to hear it.

Not everybody hears the bell, but most of us are *capable* of hearing it. We get in trouble when, for various reasons, we choose not to listen. Or maybe the bell rings, but you wish it hadn't, so you rationalize it away. You say to yourself, "This helps them and me, too." Or more bluntly, "I could really use this money."

Maybe money—the proverbial envelope discreetly referred to as "a campaign contribution"—isn't physically visible. Maybe the attempt at undue influence is a promise that you can in the future purchase stock options at a low price, or sit on the board of a new company. To the naïve or greedy, these might sound like nothing more than smart investment opportunities.

If you don't listen for the bell.

But if you *do* stop and listen, you'll know what to do. When you hear the bell, probably you need to step back and say no. At the very least, allow yourself time for reflection.

A hard and fast rule is: if you accept a political contribution, make sure it doesn't exceed that allowed by law, *and make sure every penny is reported*. You'll save yourself a lot of grief—and public humiliation—if instead of trying to circumvent the law, you play it straight. If it doesn't pass the smell test, say no.

Say no enough times and the word gets out. Influence peddlers know you're not a player. They stop coming around.

Listening for the bell applies to all sorts of things, not just money. When something doesn't sound right, learn to listen for the bell.

I can't overemphasize how much it helps to surround yourself with a good staff that listens for the bell, too. I had the best.

In more than eight decades of living—thirty-five of them in public office—I didn't always hear every bell, but I always tried to listen.

I still do.

To J. J. Pickle
With best wishes,
Richard Nixon

*Aboard Air Force One en route to the
Arkansas-Texas national championship
football game in Fayetteville, 1969.*

CLOCKWISE FROM LOWER LEFT:

*Rep. John Hammerschmidt, President Richard
Nixon, Jake, Senator William Fulbright,
Rep. Jim Wright, Senator John McClellan,
Rep. Bob Price, Rep. George Mahon,
Rep. George Bush.*

Twenty

The Ladies Excluded

It was common knowledge in Washington that President Richard Nixon was an avid football fan. On occasion, he would even call up George Allen, coach of the Washington Redskins, and beseech Allen to tell him about the Redskins' next new play.

In the fall of 1969, the University of Texas and the University of Arkansas were tied for National College Football Champion. President Nixon invited the members of Congress from Arkansas and Texas to accompany him to the championship game in Fayetteville. Many of us gladly accepted, and then we were informed that our wives were not invited because the President didn't think there was enough room on Air Force One for both members and their wives.

This became a source of considerable discomfort for some members, myself included, because many Southern women follow football as closely as men, and they badly wanted to go. I know Beryl did. Several of the other wives were equally distraught, and somehow word leaked back to President Nixon that the wives were unhappy.

The day of the game, soon after we gentlemen boarded Air Force One in Washington and were en route, Nixon invited us into the plane's "Oval Room." On board were then-Congressman George Bush, Congressman Jim Wright, Senators John McClellan and Bill Fulbright from Arkansas, Secretary of State Henry Kissinger, Congressmen Bob Price and John Paul Hammerschmidt from Arkansas, Texas Congressman George Mahon, myself, and others.

The President greeted us and apologized for not inviting the ladies. Then he said, "But I think it will work out all right, because now you won't have to try to explain the game of football to the wives when play gets underway." We all laughed half-heartedly, thinking of the explaining we had already done at home, and would do when we got back.

The President continued, "Also, you won't have to stop and describe to the ladies some parliamentary procedure or political strategy that happened in Congress last week." Looking at each other uneasily, dutifully we laughed again.

Then the President said, "And of course, if you have a spicy story you want to share, you can relax and tell it in comfort." This time we responded with the weakest of chuckles.

And then all at once, nobody said anything. It was one of those sudden moments of dead air that fill people with discomfort and make you long to think of something—anything—to say. For some reason it seemed to me that the President was staring in my direction, and I said the first thing that popped into my mind, which was, "Mr. President, my wife said to tell you that it was all right. She said she didn't vote for you in the first place!"

Everyone burst into laughter—except President Nixon, who smiled faintly and nodded, whereupon all the laughter ceased as abruptly as if strangled by garrote, and there was again awkward silence.

We flew to Fayetteville and enjoyed the game—which Texas won—but there were no further comments from the President about the compatibility of ladies and football.

Confessions
of a Rattlesnake
Chili Champ

I used to call myself Pack Mule Pickle, because I was always hauling something back and forth between Texas and Washington. One of the first things I hauled back to Washington after I was elected to Congress was venison from a deer hunt in South Texas. Texans like to brag about how they love HOT chili, a "Texas bowl of red." I made chili out of that venison, and served a special meal for members at the Texas Democratic Leadership's weekly luncheon, in Speaker John McCormack's private dining room. But I didn't make the chili *too* hot, because thirty years ago chili was still an exotic taste on the Eastern Seaboard. Of course, *my* chili was very popular! So much so that some of my Republican friends learned about it and complained about being left out. The next year I made a larger serving to include them. By this time word had spread all over the Hill. Before I knew it, my "bowls of red" had become an annual tradition on either Texas Independence Day (March 2) or San Jacinto Day (April 21).

Whenever I served chili, I tried to get Texas Congressman Kika de la Garza from Mission, Texas, to make a speech commemorating the glorious occasion when our ancestors became Texans, and Kika—a tenth-generation Texan of Hispanic descent—would grin and say, "I'm not sure you Gringos qualify!" One year he did consent to stand and give a spirited "El Grito," the Mexican cry for independence. If my chili didn't cause people's scalps to prickle, Kika's high-pitched "Ay-yi-yi-yi-yi!" did for sure.

Now all this took a lot of venison, much more than I could legally shoot. I began begging friends to donate venison to my cause. By this time, every member of the House of Representatives and the press gallery expected chili in the members' private dining room. Finally, I supplied free chili to anyone in the House of Representatives restaurant who asked for it.

The demand grew so great that on chili day lines formed outside the dining room and stretched down the hall. The House restaurant managers complained. All that free chili hurt the sale of food on the menu; some people ordered a second or third bowl, but didn't order anything else. Members tied up in committee or conference sent staff members over with a small bucket—for venison chili.

My last years in Congress I gave up trying to keeping score and served free chili to all comers. That amounted to about 1,500 individual helpings, or 250–300 pounds of venison. I never could have done it without the help of Bartel Zachry, Al Brothers, and Louis Stumberg, from the Zachry Ranch in South Texas. When they culled the deer at the end of the season, they furnished me with enough venison for my annual feast.

The chili business was a lot of work, especially for my staffers Randy Allen and Molly Kellogg, who got stuck with the chili fest every year. The venison had to be processed, flown to Washington, where it was refrigerated—but not too long!—and, finally, cooked. Randy Allen went to a restaurant supply store in Washington and bought huge plastic tubs, which we reused every year.

Of course, I didn't cook three hundred pounds of chili myself. I paid the chef and kitchen staff at the House restaurant to cook and serve it. It took the entire staff, and the entire kitchen. We used Wick Fowler's 3-Alarm Chili Mix. We didn't serve 4-Alarm, because we knew the Yankees couldn't handle it.

Thus I became known as the "Chili Champ." In the early 1980s I was asked to participate in a Congressional Chili Cookoff, and I accepted. Naturally, I wanted to do something different, so I made the mistake of bragging that *this* year, I was going to cook rattlesnake chili. Once I had said it, I couldn't take it back.

But where could we get rattlesnake meat? It wasn't an item you could pick up at Giant Food. Then I remembered that Taylor, Texas, has an annual Rattlesnake Roundup, so I asked my district administrator, Reg Todd, to contact fellows in Taylor about supplying me with the meat. Reg went to the Rattlesnake Roundup—which was one of his more unusual duties as administrator—and negotiated for several snake carcasses.

Then Reg packed the snakes in dry ice and took the box to the Austin Municipal Airport. There were a lot of people in line; holding the box, Reg joined them. When he got to the head of the line, the ticket agent asked what was in the box, and Reg said, "Rattlesnakes." People stepped back and gave him plenty of room! Finally, a man standing behind him asked why in the world was he shipping rattlesnakes? and Reg lowered his voice and said confidentially, "Well, Congressman Pickle gets real hungry for rattlesnake meat about once a month, so I have to send him a shipment."

Somewhere out there in this world is a person who thinks Jake Pickle is a peculiar man indeed.

When the rattlesnake shipment arrived, I took it home and asked Beryl to help me cook the chili. Right quick she told me she wasn't GOING TO HAVE ANYTHING TO DO WITH COOKING RATTLESNAKE CHILI! and she went to bed.

There I was in the kitchen, alone with my ambition. The rattlesnakes had been skinned, but the meat was still on the skeletons. Each snake was a white, slippery rope. First, I tried to scrape the meat off the bone. But that didn't work, because rattlesnake flesh is tenacious. It's more like mucus than meat.

Finally I woke Beryl and asked for advice. She took pity on me and suggested I parboil the meat first, so it would peel off the bone.

So I did, and that worked better. But it was slow going. Every once in a while Beryl would come to the door of the kitchen in her robe and look at me. Around midnight, I decided I'd had enough of Jake's rattlesnake chili, and the next time she appeared in the door I told Beryl I was going to bed. Later, she got to feeling guilty, got up, went into the kitchen, and, with great distaste, finished the job.

But there wasn't enough meat to make the big batch I needed. So Beryl threw in a can of Wolf Brand chili to flesh out the recipe. On impulse—or maybe for revenge—she left a couple of whole rattlesnakes in the bottom of the pot.

The next night at the big Congressional Chili Cookoff I tried to get my fellow members of Congress to sample Jake's Rattlesnake Chili. Everybody hoo-hawed. They didn't believe it was rattlesnake. Finally, I fished around in the pot with the spoon, scooped up a snake from the bottom and held it aloft. "See?"

They were aghast and drew back. But one by one, as they had a few drinks, they gathered the courage to taste it. As the evening wore on, everybody wanted some of my chili, each person daring the other to eat more. It was such a popular dish, and the "special ingredient" in the bottom of the pot—which I held up at intervals—so convincing, I won the contest.

The *New York Times* was covering the event. The next day the *Times* ran a picture of me in my chef's hat, proclaiming me Texas' "rattlesnake chili champion."

The *Times* reporter asked what was the secret to my recipe. I leaned over and said, "It's got a special BITE!" and grabbed her arm. She jumped, dropped her pad, and headed for the door.

Twenty-two

Tax Exempts:
Charities or
Tax Dodges?

When a nonprofit charity is formed and approved by the IRS, the government gives it an exemption from federal taxes. The section of the U.S. tax code which grants exemptions is referred to as 501(c)(3). In addition, 501(c)(3)s are broken down into categories: if it's a social or welfare organization, it's a 501(c)(4), if a labor, agricultural or horticultural organization, a 501(c)(5), and if a business league, trade or chamber of commerce, a 501(c)(6).

For purposes of simplification, I'll refer to tax-exempt organizations in general as 501(c)(3)s.

U.S. tax laws require, among other things, that "no part of a 501(c)(3) organization's net earnings inure to the benefit of any private shareholder or individual." Inurement is just another term for personal profit.

That sounds pretty simple, and it ought to be. But the intent of the law gets misinterpreted or goes unenforced. Many tax-exempt organizations are taking advantage of our tax laws to make a profit, and expand in ways unintended by Congress.

Tax-exempt organizations are an extremely important aspect of the U.S. tax code. They do a better job of delivering help to the needy than the federal government. And that is their purpose: to give charities a break. But there is an urgent need for legislative reform to address self-dealing in public charities. Self-dealing is activities by which "insiders" (officers, directors, managers, or trustees in a position to control expenditures of tax-exempt charities) give themselves, or others, special salaries or expenses.

Clamping down on tax-exempt abuse will mean complete reform measures, including enforcement of the Unrelated Business Income Tax (UBIT)—taxes an organization should pay on "offshoot" income (income not a direct result of its charitable function). Because it's such an emotional issue that affects so many people, both Democrats and Republicans have been unwilling to tackle the problem.

In 1995 there were over 1.4 million tax-exempt organizations in the United States, nearly half of which are Section 501(c)(3) public charities. It's estimated that an additional 358,000 churches are also tax exempt under Section 501(c)(3). And these numbers are growing. In one year alone an additional forty thousand organizations were granted tax-exempt status!

Tax exempts are big business. The most recent Internal Revenue Service data shows that in 1994 public charities had revenues of *$554 billion*—a whopping 8 percent of the Gross National Product, up from 3.5 percent in 1975. Over the same period, the assets of public charities grew from $108 billion to $890 billion.

U.S. tax laws say that an organization is qualified to receive tax-deductible contributions and is exempt from most federal taxes if:

+ No part of the organization's earnings benefit a private individual.

+ The organization does not participate in political campaigns.

+ The organization does not engage in substantial lobbying or other attempts to influence legislation.

These laws are clear and unmistakable. Regrettably, they are not being strictly enforced.

In 1987, the IRS suggested that the Oversight Committee, a subcommittee of the House Ways and Means Committee, look into tax-exempt organizations. The Oversight Committee studies the fairness and function of U.S. tax laws. So the Oversight Committee—of which I was chairman—held a series of hearings to examine three areas of tax-exempt organizations: lobbying and political activities, activities that produce UBIT, and television ministries. The goal of our hearings was to determine whether certain organizations were operating in a manner that merited federal tax exemption—and public trust.

Perhaps the most controversial aspect of these hearings was our investigation into charities and television ministries. Our hearings stirred up a hornet's nest of resentment from organizations which thought they were exempt from *any* public investigation. Actually, there had been no Congressional inquiry into tax exempts for over twenty years. Lulled by the lack of scrutiny, some organizations had grown complacent or self dealing.

The Oversight Committee requested information from the Independent Sector, the trade association for nonprofit organizations. Scheduled to appear before us was their spokesperson, Marion R. Fremont-Smith. When I asked what type of organization she represented and how much federal income tax its members paid, she said that information was *private* and *privileged*, and only the IRS had the right to request it. Throughout our questioning, she was so evasive that in exasperation I said that what information she was giving us was like striking a match in Carlsbad Caverns—it didn't illuminate very much!

Finally, Oversight indicated that we had no choice but to subpoena the Independent Sector's tax records and make them public. Suddenly, we had their attention! Later, we got an apology from the organization, and they began to cooperate and clean up their tax abuses. But in the beginning, they were hostile to what they saw as attempts to curtail their power.

Many television ministers were hostile as well. Prior to the opening of Oversight's hearings, the media began speculating that Congress was "out to get the evangelists." So, in an attempt to reassure everybody that we were not singling out a particular group, we requested a pre-hearing meeting with many of the country's prominent television ministers.

As I remember, those who accepted our invitation to the meeting were Jerry Falwell (*Old Time Gospel Hour*); Jimmy Swaggart (the Jimmy Swaggart Ministries) and his wife, Francie; John Ankerberg (the *John Ankerberg Show*); and Paul Crouch (with Trinity Broadcasting). Robert Tilton, Ernest Angsley, and Jim and Tammy Faye Bakker either didn't respond or declined to participate. The Reverend Dr. Billy Graham was out of the country at the time of the hearings. However, Dr. Graham said he had nothing to hide and volunteered to let the committee examine his ministry's records.

At the preliminary meeting, Francie Swaggart did most of the talking. She made it plain: we had no business looking into *her* business. Rev. Swaggart didn't say much. Studying his hands and the table, he was good cop to Francie's bad cop. She wore a lot of gold jewelry; he wore a gold ring set with a Texas-size diamond.

The morning of the hearing, we needed to put the television ministers in a room before the hearing started, while they waited to testify. Given their celebrity status, they didn't want to be hanging around in the hall like nobodies and common criminals. We offered them Room 1129 of the Longworth Office Building. They said that was satisfactory, *except* that they didn't want to wait in the same room with Oral Roberts! Roberts had recently and very publicly announced that he had just "come down from the Tower," where he had talked with God, who had told Roberts he would die if he didn't raise more money. I don't know whether the other ministers were reluctant to be associated with Roberts—or afraid of heavenly wrath. In any case, they refused to wait in fellowship with him.

So we segregated the other television ministers from Oral Roberts, who sat alone in the office of Beth Vance, Oversight's legal counsel. It was rather pathetic. Roberts seemed like a lost, sweet man.

The Oversight Committee did not swear in the ministers when they testified before us. Making ministers take an oath made a lot of committee members nervous; they thought it was a hard-line approach and bad public relations for Congress. All of us were getting angry phone calls and letters from folks stirred up over our "persecution" of clergymen, so I didn't insist on an oath. In retrospect, I should have insisted. What we got from the evangelists was vague testimony and promises that they would police themselves in the future. In all honesty, I don't think their taking an oath would have made a bit of difference. But it would have made me feel better.

During our hearings, I became concerned about a fund-raising letter that the National Religious Broadcasters sent to its membership, castigating our hearings and calling our committee "the enemy we need to fight." I've always wondered how much money they raised with that sleazy newsletter. I should have asked the Justice Department to check it out. The National Religious Broadcasters conveniently overlooked the fact that they were an organization dedicated to good will and to telling the truth.

Our committee did succeed in tightening up the law on lobbying and focusing attention on inurement. Jerry Falwell finally admitted that the ministries should police themselves more carefully, and that there should be better security in the area of tax-exempt income. "When we compete with free enterprise, we should be listed as FOR PROFIT and pay taxes," Falwell said.

Well, that'll be the day, I thought. I haven't noticed that happening yet, and that was years ago.

What are the abuses in the area of inurement? Our committee staff, including Susan Athey and Pat Heck, audited the tax data of two hundred of the largest tax-exempt organizations in the United States. Here's a small sample of our findings:

- A CEO of a health organization received a salary of over $1 million, with added benefits.

- Another health organization was family controlled, with all kinds of expensive deductions, including vacations and leased vehicles. Moreover, the minutes of their board meeting were falsified! After an IRS audit, the organization simply paid a fine and kept right on operating. Essentially, they received no more than a slap on the wrist. Their charter was not voided.

- A television minister held extravagant receptions and had an island vacation home. One minister paid his home mortgage from ministry funds without board approval.

- Another television minister used the services of an exclusive fund-raiser. Virtually all the money raised was spent on the fund-raiser, and very little given to the poor.

- The president of a university received an annual salary of $365,000, plus a $1 million loan ($500,000 to buy his home, and $500,000 to remodel it).

- Four trustees of an educational assistance charity were each paid almost $700,000 a year—for two meetings!

- One university spent $600,000 in one year to hire a lobbyist; two other universities spent $650,000 for the SAME lobbyist.

These are just a few examples of the shocking abuses that were taking place in tax-exempt organizations a decade ago. Many organizations were engaging in the "Great Tax Dodge."

First, our committee addressed the questions on unrelated business wrongs. After the Oversight hearings in 1987, we drafted a UBIT bill and presented it to the Ways and Means Committee. However, we couldn't get approval from the Reagan-Bush administrations, which were influenced by pressure from constituents and interest groups such as the Christian Coalition. We sent the bill to the Treasury Department and asked for Treasury's support. The Assistant Secretary of the Treasury, Ken Gideon, wrote back, "We cannot support any changes now." The issue died down, but didn't go away.

In 1991, reporter Diane Sawyer interviewed me for the ABC-television program *Prime Time*, which was investigating allegations of abuse by television evangelists, in particular Robert Tilton and Larry Lea. The show aired film clips of the children's mission in Haiti supposedly funded by Tilton and Lea—who switched the sign out front depending on which ministry was due to visit or needed photographs for promotional brochures. Also shown were some of Tilton's disillusioned viewers, weeping as they described how the prayer requests they'd sent to Tilton were opened by a clearinghouse and thrown into a dumpster.

During the ABC taping, Sawyer asked me, "Congressman, what action do you intend to take?" and I wished I had a better answer for her, but I told her that we had referred our committee's findings to the IRS for investigation. At that point, there wasn't much more we could do.

However, the IRS did begin auditing television and other ministries more vigorously. Today, Oversight receives quarterly reports on pending IRS investigations into tax exempts, especially television ministers.

Because of stricter audits, several television ministers were eventually fined or sent to prison. Also, knowing the IRS might be watching has made tax exempts more accountable.

The shenanigans of television ministers had another side effect, one I take personally: evangelists helped make white shoes and white belts unfashionable! I always liked a crisp white belt and matching shoes, so I'm mad at evangelists for ruining a perfectly good look.

We could not get any action on the UBIT matter—there was just too much opposition from the top and an unwillingness on the part of Treasury to proceed. However, during our hearings, Treasury specifically asked Congress to look into the inurement question and pass legislation to correct abuse. We did so the next session of Congress, by recommending strong measures in a bill unanimously passed by our Oversight Committee and then the full Ways and Means Committee.

The bill we passed out of Ways and Means provided a 25 percent excise tax for abuses. However, the House couldn't consider it: we had no legislation to which we could attach our bill. We tried to attach it to the General Agreement on Trade and Tariffs (GATT) legislation, but Senate conferees Pat Moynihan and Bob Packwood refused, saying it was too controversial and would "slow down" or hurt the chance of GATT's passage. They suggested we wait and introduce the bill the next session of Congress.

Actually, I suspect that blatant lobbying by Sloan/Kettering, Kodak, Yale, Harvard, and Stanford Universities killed the bill. I met with Moynihan and Packwood, trying to convince them. In frustration, I told them a story about my father, and how he had pushed me to pass a civil rights bill thirty years before. At the time I told him, "Pop, your generation and others didn't do a thing about civil rights, and all of a sudden you expect us to rectify the injustices of two hundred years—overnight! We can't do it that fast, but we'll get there in fifteen or twenty years."

And Pop, who was in his eighties, said, "No sir, I haven't got time to wait! You've got to do it now, while I'm here to see it happen!"

Moynihan and Packwood laughed at this story, but they were unmoved. Finally, Moynihan reached across the conference table and offered his hand. "Jake, I give you my word. We'll get it done next year. I promise!" he said, and we shook.

I'm still waiting.

In the meantime, have tax-exempt abuses stopped? *Are* organizations policing themselves?

Sadly, not much. Abuses are still being exposed. In 1989, the Bishop Estate Trustees who manage the Kamehameha Schools in Hawaii received $681,763 per year salary *each*. The Kamehameha Schools invested in shopping centers, apparel chains, and drilling ventures. They don't pay taxes; they reinvest—and get bigger and bigger. That's true of many big charities.

It's too bad journalists or the public don't more closely examine the Form 990 forms submitted to the IRS by tax-exempt organizations. The 990 is a tax-exempt organization's equivalent of the average citizen's 1040. Form 990 data is available without charge to anyone who wants to know how tax-exempt organizations make and spend their money.

Who *are* the organizations which abuse the law? It's more than just a few insiders; it's nearly everybody. Typical 501(c)(3) abusers are hospitals, health care organizations, museums, public radio and television, golf courses, country clubs, private boarding schools, colleges, universities, cemeteries, labor unions, trade organizations, public hearing agencies, festivals, bar associations, operas, credit unions, scouting organizations, local chambers of commerce, symphonies, clubs, nursing homes . . . you name it. Of course, not every member of the listed groups is an abuser. But many are.

A common misconception is that nonprofits *don't make a profit*. Many of them do! However, tax-exempt organizations' profit is called net income—and it is not returned to investors.

The reality is that we have made little headway reversing the failure of many nonprofit organizations to pay UBIT taxes or correct inurement abuse. So far, every administration has essentially looked the other way. In October 1995, *U.S. News and World Report* ran a special issue showing how abuses continue to occur. It created a ripple in Congress, but not much more. Somebody ought to do something. Nonprofits are creating subsidiaries *for profit* at a rapid rate. Little tax is being paid, and there is little control of inurement and salaries. It has become common for nonprofit organizations to attract top management with salaries of $1–3 million dollars a year. *Their* charity begins at home.

For instance, the financial investment officer at Harvard University is being paid $2.9 million a year, because Harvard says it must pay big salaries in order to compete with business. Meanwhile, the National Federation of Independent Businesses and other trade associations adopt an adversarial, self-righteous stance. NFIB would rather make headlines by opposing a tax bill proposed by a Democratic President than protest the abuses of tax-exempt organizations.

Remember: tax-exempt organizations are growing at the rate of more than forty thousand *a year*. Most are small, but the Big Boys—research, health, colleges and universities, safety testing agencies, hospitals, and ministries—are expanding at an astonishing rate. Someday, unless a course of action is formulated, the tax exempts will be so large that no one can touch them. Some are that big now.

What can be done?

- Do more audits.

- When a violation is not corrected, the Justice Department should prosecute—quickly.

- The U.S. Treasury should scrutinize all 501(c)(3) applications, and members of Congress must be more cautious about recommending candidates for tax-exempt status.

- UBIT and inurement laws must be strengthened and enforced.

- Nationally, we need to adopt a stricter attitude about tax exempts. The Treasury Department and the IRS are too soft. They are afraid that by canceling a tax exempt's charter, they hurt the recipients of charity instead of the abuser. But tax abuse on this scale hurts *everybody*.

- Congress should impose a 25 percent excise tax on inurement violations. This would affect abusers where it hurts most—the bottom line.

To be honest, controlling tax exempts is a complicated problem. Colleges, universities, health researchers, museums, and other organizations deserve tax exemptions. However, some of these organizations have budgets of billions of dollars! They should pay UBIT taxes *as the law requires*, and their salaries should be reasonable.

Part of the problem is that the current U.S. tax code is so vague and riddled with exceptions that few organizations end up paying UBIT, even when they should. But as I see it, the *real* problem with reform is that nobody really *knows* what to do. Tax-exempt organizations are so prevalent, influential, and vocal that the prospect of deciding who needs reform—and how—is daunting.

So far, Congress, stung by criticism that it is mixing church and state and hurting the poor folks, has done almost nothing. As former Senator Lloyd Bentsen, who sat on the Senate Finance Committee, told me, "This tax-exempt business is a sticky wicket."

Every member of Congress graduated from a college or university, belongs to a club, sits on a foundation board, attends a church or synagogue, works for a charity—or has thousands of constituents who do. And of course, everybody wants to continue doing good.

But few charities want to pay taxes!

How Big Business Threatens Our Nation's Pension Funds

Did you know that by 1993, General Motors' pension fund was underfunded by $20 billion? If you didn't know, don't feel bad. General Motors didn't tell its employees, either!

Since the Great Depression, retirement policy in the United States has been based on the concept that workers should rely on a combination of Social Security benefits, employer-sponsored pensions, and individual savings. This is the so-called three-legged stool that supports retirement security for all workers.

Expansion of the Individual Retirement Account (IRA) and Section 401(k) employee savings programs in the early 1980s greatly strengthened the ability of workers to save for retirement. Enactment of the Social Security amendments of 1983 put the largest federal retirement program on a strong financial footing until the twenty-first century. However, by the late 1980s, the third leg of the stool—employer-sponsored pension plans—was becoming dangerously unstable.

The right of workers to receive their pensions after a lifetime of labor should be inalienable. They have contributed to their company's pension fund for thirty to forty years and, at the age of sixty or sixty-five, earned their retirement.

This wasn't always the case. Years ago, private pension funds were not protected. Discriminatory eligibility rules, financial mismanagement, and a series of plan failures caused workers to lose benefits. When Studebaker Automobile went bankrupt in 1963, 4,400 workers lost most or all of their pensions.

The Studebaker collapse was especially significant because it focused public attention on two issues: the lack of minimum funding standards and the lack of pension insurance to protect workers' benefits when a plan failed. Michael Gordon, a prominent pension expert in Washington, D.C., wrote, "The extremely rapid growth of private pension plans had led to all manner of abuses, ranging from ineptness and lack of know-how to outright looting of benefit funds and corrupt administration. In addition to embezzlements, kickbacks, unjustifiably high administrative costs, and excessive investment of funds in employer securities and excessive fees, serious examples of improper insurance practices were also found" (Ch. 1, p. 2, in *The Employee Retirement Income Security Act of 1974: The First Decade*, Congressional Document, 1984).

Many of the violations were made federal crimes. During the seventies and eighties, after investigations by Senators John McClellan (D-Ark.), Jacob Javits (D-N.Y.), John Williams (R-Del.), and Labor Secretary Willard Wirtz, it became obvious that there was a need for a bill which could set up strict federal fiduciary standards of funding, vesting, and enforcement.

In 1974, Congress passed the Employee Income Retirement Security Act (ERISA), which created the Pension Benefit Guaranty Corporation (PBGC) to help protect federally funded retirement plans. The PBGC has been of immeasurable benefit to workers. Companies pay a small premium (deductible, too!) each year for PBGC insurance, which pays benefits to workers of a defunct company. From time to time, the premium has been raised or speeded up as the economy changes.

The solvency of PBGC's pension fund depends on *all* companies paying their premiums, thereby properly funding their own plans. ERISA was created because some private companies either neglected or abused their plans. Unfortunately, some companies continued to manage their plans improperly even after ERISA was enacted. Eventually, a series of plan failures, culminating in the collapse of the Ling-Temco-Vought, Inc. (LTV) plan in 1986 placed the PBGC in financial difficulty. Increasingly, corporate raiders saw fat pension plans not as examples of fiscal responsibility but as targets for plunder. A 1991 article in the *Philadelphia Inquirer* by Donald Bartlett and James Steele (quoted in *When Corporations Rule the World* by David Korten, 1995) estimated that the new owners of two thousand U.S. companies drained what they saw as $21 billion in "excess" funding from pension funds, applying it to takeover debt repayment.

In 1987, the Oversight Committee, of which I was chairman, released its recommendations for pension reform. The committee found that the PBGC's financial condition had steadily deteriorated, despite past increases in the insurance premium. This continued deterioration was the direct result of the termination of seriously underfunded pension plans, particularly in the steel industry. The demise of just three steel industry plans was responsible for more than 60 percent of the PBGC's $4 billion deficit.

This trend by a relatively few employers toward maintaining increasingly underfunded pension plans not only threatened the solvency of the PBGC, but also denied workers their promised retirement security. Moreover, it unfairly shifted that burden to the vast majority of employers who operated well-funded pension plans.

To address these problems, the Oversight Committee recommended that:

- Employers should be required to fund their plans more rapidly.

- When terminating an underfunded plan, employers must be liable for the full amount of the underfunding.

- Sponsors of underfunded plans must pay an additional insurance premium to the PBGC, based on the level of plan underfunding.

These recommendations served as the foundation for the Pension Protection Act (PPA) of 1987 and were adopted as part of the Omnibus Budget Reconciliation Act of 1987.

The PPA did not address the immediate financial problems facing the PBGC. Unfortunately, the PPA reforms proved inadequate to address the underlying problem of pension underfunding. Companies continued to use loopholes in ERISA to avoid their pension obligations. By 1992, it was obvious that without legislation this trend would continue indefinitely, leading to ever larger pension failures. On July 28, 1992, Secretary of Labor Lynn Martin, testifying before the Ways and Means Committee, called on Congress once again to repair the pension safety net, saying: "Congress has the opportunity to show it has learned the painful lesson taught us by the Savings & Loan fiasco by taking the necessary steps now to fix the Pension Benefit Guaranty Corporation. The time to act is now before another crisis occurs."

The Bush administration proposed four major reforms: stronger funding requirements for underfunded pension plans, limited PGBC guarantees for benefit increases in underfunded pension plans, enhanced priority for the PBGC's claims in bankruptcy proceedings, and reforms to reflect the PBGC's financial effect on the federal budget.

Some of our largest and most respected companies, especially in the airline, automobile, tire, rubber, and steel industries, failed to pay their premiums. The unfunded liability of our pension funds was over $53 billion at the end of 1992, growing to $71 billion by December 31, 1993. Obviously, in an economic depression, the PBGC wouldn't have the funds to pay workers. This meant that Uncle Sam probably would have to bail out the system by paying workers' pensions. Thus, the potential risk to every taxpayer was great.

It is shocking that many of the United States' biggest and "best" companies have deliberately chosen to spend their money on activities other than meeting their pension liabilities. Here is a list of some top U.S. companies which were delinquent in 1993:

ACF Industries/TWA	$689 million
Uniroyal Goodrich Tire	$532 million
Kaiser Aluminum	$352 million
Northwest Airlines, Inc.	$647 million
National Steel Corp.	$448 million
CSX Corp.	$313 million
US Air Group	$573 million
Goodyear Tire & Rubber	$388 million
Reynolds Metals Co.	$283 million
Honeywell Inc.	$434 million

United Technologies	$799 million
Inland Steel Industries, Inc.	$384 million
Unisys	$324 million
General Motors Corp.	$19.5 billion
LTV Corporation	$2.2 billion
Bethlehem Steel Corp.	$1.9 billion
Westinghouse Electric	$2 billion

The list goes on and on. At the time, fifty companies accounted for $40 billion of the country's $53 billion in unfunded plans. The pension underfunding of these fifty companies represents about 56 percent of the underfunding in single employer plans.

It should be noted that 85 percent of the pension plans in the United States *were* properly funded. This means that 85 percent of companies were paying their premiums—and protecting the pension plans of the irresponsible 15 percent *not* paying premiums!

Our Oversight Committee held hearings and began drafting a bill to strengthen rules to better protect workers, retirees, and the PBGC. Our efforts were supported by the Bush administration and the PBGC. When we asked the Treasury and Labor Departments for suggestions, they responded decisively. Secretary of Labor Lynn Martin and James Lockhart, the head of the PBGC, urged corrections.

When Bill Clinton was elected President in 1992, Secretary of Labor Robert Reich, supported by Secretary of the Treasury Lloyd Bentsen, Executive Director of the PBGC Marty Slate, and Office of Management and Budget Director Leon Panetta, began to work on the problem. An inter-agency task force drafted a reform bill and asked Oversight to help pass it. The reform bill was similar to Oversight's recommendations, and we agreed to adopt their approach, although it wasn't as tough as I would have liked—an opinion shared by Rep. Amo Houghton (R-N.J.), the ranking Republican member on the Oversight Committee, and by Oversight staffer Joseph Grant.

However, the opposition to the legislation by big business was horrendous! They wanted to use pension money for salaries, bonuses, equipment, and current expenses. They claimed their pension funds were in great shape, with better value than we had estimated. They used estimated interest rates on earnings that were higher than a cat's back. They used mortality rates that were inconsistent and at times outrageous.

The power of these big companies was considerable. Yet the hard, cold fact remained: the United States had an unfunded pension fund liability of over $53 billion. We had to act, and quickly.

A group of lobbyists representing big companies appealed to Treasury Secretary Lloyd Bentsen, asking him to go slow and give them more time. Secretary Bentsen told them politely but firmly, "You fellows must pay up. I used to be in the insurance business, and I know how you're abusing the interest rate and mortality assumptions."

The truth of the matter is that average workers have little evidence that their particular pension fund is solvent. If they ask their company about it, chances are they will be told everything is fine. Most workers take their company's word for it.

At one of our hearings in 1993, Marvin Clarke, a retiree of the Hanlin Group, Moundsville, West Virginia, testified how badly he had been hurt. Clark was an employee of the Hanlin Chemical company in West Virginia for thirty-five years. The company became bankrupt, and Clarke's pension was cut by 35 percent. He lost $700 per month—for the rest of his life. "I had the American dream," said Clarke. "I never was laid off. I always had a paycheck, and never had to apply for assistance or food stamps, never had to ask anyone for help, always paid my taxes with a smile. Now I've lost my entire savings. I've lost most of my pension, and all this has affected my health, causing me additional problems. What have I done wrong?"

At another hearing, a former pilot for Eastern Airlines, Eilert "Buster" Moldenhauer, pointed out how the sale of Eastern by Frank Borman to the Frank Lorenzo Group (which ended in bankruptcy) broke the airline's promise to its employees. The PBGC was unable to pay full benefits. Moldenhauer testified, "After all the legal dust had settled, I found out that I lost almost half of the benefits promised me."

He concluded, "Gentlemen, please don't listen to the so-called experts when they tell you that additional reform is not needed. My case is a shining example to the contrary . . . the important ideas and concepts incorporated into ERISA almost twenty years ago have not yet been fully implemented."

We listened to many other people testify that their pension plans had been insolvent, and the PBGC unable to cover them. We could see that the law needed to be changed.

Oversight passed the administration's bill out of committee in 1994. Rep. Bill Ford (D-Mich.), House Chairman, Education and Labor Committee, later passed essentially the same bill. However, we had no tax bill to which to attach our pension reform measure.

Then a break came from an unexpected source: the General Agreement on Trade and Tariffs Bill (GATT). To finance GATT, the administration needed to find $12 billion in offsetting revenues over a five-year period. Any loss in federal revenues (which GATT would cause in some areas) would be offset on a dollar-for-dollar basis. The proposed pension fund legislation endorsed by the Clinton administration would go a long way toward raising the revenue, while at the same time passing a much-needed pension reform bill.

At first, I didn't like the idea of combining a pension reform bill with a trade bill. I wanted our bill to go to the House floor, where we might strengthen the measure. I thought we had given underfunded companies too much time to pay up, and too much wiggle room on interest rates. High interest rate assumptions let companies reduce the money they had to contribute to their plans.

However, our bill did lift the premium payment cap for underfunded plans, speed up the payment of premiums, and provide better notice to beneficiaries. It was a compromise all around. As Assistant Secretary of Treasury Les Samuels said, "The administration got 90 percent of what it wanted in long-term reform, and the companies got a longer time to comply."

So we agreed to place the Pension Reform Act into the GATT bill. It was a wonderful wedding! GATT passed with our amendment. Frankly, I doubt if we could have passed pension reform in 1994 as a free-standing bill.

Prior to the passage of the Pension Reform Act, PBGC was listed by the General Accounting Office as a "high risk agency"—an agency that could go broke. By early 1995 that danger was past, and the General Accounting Office gave the PBGC a clean bill of health. The bill's passage was due in part to the hard work of Marty Slate, Les Samuels,

Joseph Grant, Mildred Worrell, counsel to the Committee on Ways and Means, and my colleague Amo Houghton.

In retrospect, I took considerable pride in knowing that the Oversight Committee had taken the first step toward passing a reform bill in 1987 and a second pension bill in 1994. On behalf of Oversight, I received a letter of thanks from President Clinton, in which he called the "Passage of the Retirement Protection Act of 1994 one of the major accomplishments of the 103rd Congress."

Of course, not everybody was happy with some of the bill's changes, especially lump sum retirement payments, and limitations for 401(k)s. One Dallas geologist was furious, and was quoted in the *Wall Street Journal* saying, "Which of our dadgummed Congressmen put THAT in? We need to string him up from the highest tree!" One of my staffers left the article on my desk. In the margin he had scribbled, "Pickle—that's you!"

Today, the struggle to protect pensions continues.

In 1995, in the House Reconciliation Bill, the Republicans put in a provision allowing companies to remove tens of billions of dollars of "surplus" assets from pension plans and to use them for any purpose: to pay executive bonuses, buy equipment—even finance hostile takeovers! This provision would have reversed the progress made under the Pension Reform Bill. Fortunately, by a vote of 94 to 5, the Senate voted against that change in late 1995. But that provision was included by the conferees in a budget reform bill vetoed by President Clinton. As of March 1996, it is uncertain whether the provision will surface again.

President Clinton is aware how vigilant we must be to keep safeguards in place. Speaking to a group of labor leaders in October 1995, he said, "In the 1980s, when thousands and thousands of corporations transferred some $20 billion out of their employees' pension funds for buy-outs and other purposes, an awful lot of workers lost their life savings. Last December, one of the things I am proudest of . . . was the fact that Congress passed a bill that saved 8.5 million pensions, and stabilized 40 million other pensions in danger. This (Republican) budget would allow companies to withdraw money from their workers' pension funds, and use it for whatever reason they want. Say no to that proposal. Say no to looting pension funds. Say no. It's wrong."

So far, Congress has listened.

In retrospect, it seems that much of my Congressional career has been spent protecting the retirement income security of working Americans. I was on the House Foreign Commerce Committee, the Oversight and Investigations Committee, and, later, the Ways and Means Committee. I didn't plan it that way, but events and conditions were thrust upon me. Some highlights I find worth remembering:

- My first efforts in the late 1960s resulted in forcing International Telephone and Telegraph (ITT-Hartford) to pay $20 million in taxes on corporate assets. Michael Keeling, then my staff legal counsel (and now President of the national Employee Stock Option Plan) brought these abuses to my attention.

- I led the fight to clean up corruption in the Central States Teamsters Pension Fund during the seventies and eighties. With cooperation from the Department of Labor, we passed a bill that greatly controlled the administration and investment of the Teamsters' fund. Secretary of Labor Ray Marshall led efforts to finalize better control over the Teamsters fund.

- I was Chairman of the Social Security Subcommittee when we passed the 1983 Social Security Reform Bill, legislation that helped insure the solvency of the Social Security System.

- In 1984, my Oversight Committee passed the Disability Reform Bill. At the time, thousands of beneficiaries were being knocked off disability rolls, and we needed to protect them with new legislation. I give much credit to Erv Hytner, Oversight's legal counsel, who redrafted controversial sections into language everyone could accept. Senator Bob Dole agreed to crucial provisions, and we got a Disability Bill passed.

- In 1987, my Oversight Committee passed the Pension Protection Act, and in 1994, the historic Pension Reform Act.

In every one of these fights the odds were against us as we fought powerful interests. It wasn't easy. Sometimes national interests conflicted with Texas interests. I remember a 1987 meeting with a representative of LTV, who wanted me to roll back the date on the Pension Reform bill, thus granting LTV's troubled pension fund a billion-dollar exemption. I refused, because it would have been unfair to other companies. During that fight I remember that Ways and Means Chairman Dan Rostenkowski announced in conference that committee member Jake Pickle didn't want the date rolled back, and Senator Bentsen supported me. Like me, Bentsen—a Texan—would have liked to help LTV. But we couldn't make exceptions.

In every struggle, I sought cooperation from Republican allies—not just ranking members of a committee, but members with low seniority. It takes both parties to pass a bill.

When we started work on the Pension Reform Bill, (Republican) Secretary of Labor Lynn Martin recommended changes, then criticized the Democratic Congress for "dragging its feet." The AFL-CIO opposed the bill and accused the Republicans of "scaremongering." Then President Clinton was elected, and a new administration had to be educated all over again on the issue of pension reform.

In the end, Democrats supported the bill as much as Republicans. And what started out as a priority for the Bush administration ended up as one of President Clinton's most valued achievements.

Each of the retirement income security bills for which I fought protects the interest of average working Americans. Each was passed on a bipartisan basis in the public eye, and paid for without gimmicks, shortcuts, or legislative sleight-of-hand. I like to think each bill will have a positive, long-lasting impact on millions of Americans who will never know of its existence. In my own Texas district, I doubt many constituents realize I was prominently involved in pension fund legislation.

The danger we face is that, inevitably, some corporations will continue wanting to raid their pension funds, to use them as enormous floating crap games to dip into at will. Experience has shown us that pension funds raided and "invested" have been at risk—or lost—while the federal government has picked up the tab, at great expense to the taxpayer. The lure of the pension fund hen house is so appealing, the corporate fox can't always resist. We must see that he does.

When President Clinton signed the Retirement Protection Act in 1994 in a White House ceremony, he said, "I'd like to thank someone who's not here today—my friend Jake Pickle, who is retiring from Congress, and left this act as a legacy in a long career of helping people with their lives."

Ahhhhh, that's worth the fight! Thank you, Mr. President.

*Vice President Al Gore autographs Jake's
antique pump organ in a hallway of the
U.S. Capitol while Pickle staffer
Molly Kellogg watches, 1994.*

Congressional
Prayer
Breakfasts

Over forty years ago, Senators Frank Carlson (R-Kans.) and Price Daniel (D-Tex.) led a campaign to provide a nondenominational "prayer room" in the nation's Capitol, where members of Congress could pray, count their blessings, and ask God for guidance. It's customary for an attendant to stand outside the prayer room, so that any member who has retreated to talk to his or her God won't be disturbed or lobbied. There are times when the prayer room seems to be the only place on Capitol Hill where a member of Congress can find solitude.

The House and Senate hold separate weekly prayer services, and both houses hold a joint prayer breakfast in January at the Washington Hilton Hotel, at the opening of each session of Congress. The President of the United States is special guest, and a prominent national figure is principal speaker. It's a big event, drawing as many as four thousand people, and it's a hopeful way to start the year. Early in the session tempers are cool and spirits high. The members look at each other, and it seems possible to accomplish good things.

But since the 1950s, the House has had a smaller, more intimate tradition. At 8 A.M. every Thursday when Congress is in session, the House prayer group meets in room H-122 for Continental breakfast. It's a bipartisan group, limited to members of Congress only. That makes everyone feel free. Once a member, always a member. Even retired representatives like me come back.

Prayer breakfasts are open to all members of the House; usually thirty to fifty show up. It's a loyal and caring group, a gathering of ordinary men and women who are asked to do extraordinary things, and need God's guidance. I didn't make every prayer breakfast because sometimes I had meetings, or was in Texas, but I was a regular attendee. Some members wouldn't miss it.

The prayer breakfast is opened with a reading from Scripture. Then there's a "chaplain's report" given by Congressman G. V. ("Sonny") Montgomery (D-Miss.). The chaplain's report is like the "Joys and Concerns" part of a church service: it mentions members who are ill, in difficulty, or celebrating a triumph. Sonny has been making this report for thirty years. He does an excellent job of gathering personal information about our members—"our family." I think he runs for re-election just so he can attend our prayer breakfast and give his chaplain's report.

After that, we sing a hymn, usually selected by former Rep. Charles Whitley (D-N.C.), now a Washington lobbyist. As introduction, Whitley always says, "But before we sing, I yield to the gentleman from Texas. Three minutes!"

I always get three minutes, and I always take it, too!

My job is to tell the background of the hymn Whitley has chosen. Who was the author, and what inspired him? I've always thought the *stories* behind the hymns are as interesting as the songs themselves, and often more inspiring than any sermon.

I don't know how I got started doing this, but I've been doing it off and on for thirty years. It's become a hobby; I own a dozen books about the histories of hymns. I was hooked the first time I read about "Amazing Grace," written by Englishman John Newton. Newton was a slave trader who repented his sins, went back to Olney, England, became a minister, and wrote what is surely one of the world's most moving songs.

By now, I know most of the stories by heart and can tell them without preparation. Sometimes the members think I'm making up the story! Jim Ford, the House chaplain and a close friend, teases me by asking, "Pickle, are you telling the truth?" This is the *chaplain* speaking! Some members claim my memory's TOO amazing. It's really not that amazing when you consider I've been doing it for thirty years. Besides, Whitley picks well-known, spirited hymns. We don't sing mournful hymns. We like 'em upbeat and inspiring! There are only 50–100 hymns like that. Eventually, you learn them all.

Favorite hymns sung as openers for our Congressional Prayer Breakfasts are "All Hail the Power of Jesus' Name," "Come Thou Almighty King," "Pass Me Not, Gentle Savior," "In the Garden," "Holy, Holy, Holy," "Blessed Assurance," "Revive Me Again," "The Church in the Wildwood," "Softly and Tenderly," "Blest Be the Tie That Binds," "The Old Rugged Cross," "Faith of Our Fathers," and "Shall We Gather at the River?"

After the hymn, a member of Congress is our featured speaker. Most don't talk about legislation, except when they are struggling with their conscience over a particular vote. Usually they talk about personal experiences, or how faith played a part in their lives.

These talks are always fascinating, and often moving. The members, speaking informally among friends, give an excellent accounting of their struggles, joys, ambitions, and philosophies. Some members accidentally became politicians because some pivotal event in their lives affected them so deeply they wanted to make a difference. Some are reformed alcoholics. Most, at one time in their lives, have "fallen from grace"—and risen again. They talk candidly, sometimes painfully, sharing the stories of their lives.

I was a featured speaker several times. I talked about growing up in Big Spring, Texas, and how going to Sunday School and church was automatic. Nobody said, "Are we going to church today?" We just DID. The whole family went to church, including a few times—always uninvited—my dog Rex.

I talked about working in the White House Grocery. I talked about the lessons my parents taught me. Pop would say, "Now don't talk so much you give yourself away." Mom would caution, "Jarrell, don't speak too highly of yourself." Their good advice is why I've always been so humble and meek!

On special occasions, I have transported to our Congressional Prayer Breakfasts an old pump organ. It's fire-engine red. The organ is over 100 years old and was owned by Walter and Ann Hornaday. Walter was a correspondent for the *Dallas Morning News*. He and Ann owned a farm on the Shenandoah River, near Berryville, Virginia. When the Hornadays entertained, their guests signed the red organ in bright white paint. The first time I saw it, in the 1940s, I noticed one of the biggest names right in the middle of the pedals: SAM RAYBURN. That impressed me, and I never forgot the organ.

When Walter Hornaday died, I bought the organ and had it restored by a music professor at the University of West Virginia. It still plays fine, if you pump it hard enough. Because it was part of Washington history (and because Beryl didn't want it at home!), I moved it to my office in the Cannon Office Building.

Over the years I have continued the Hornadays' tradition of having guests sign the organ. Signatures on the organ include those of Speaker Jim Wright, Governor Price Daniel, Governor John Connally, Speaker Tip O'Neill, Governor Ann Richards, Former First Lady of the United States Lady Bird Johnson, Senator Lloyd Bentsen, Speaker Tom Foley, Rep. Dick Gephardt, Senator Tom Connally, Rep. Dan Rostenkowski, Rep. Sonny Montgomery, Rep. Jack Kemp, Liz and Les Carpenter, Secretary Henry Cisneros, Rep. Henry B. Gonzalez, Rep. Sam Gibbons, Rep. Charles Rangel, Rep. Jack Brooks, Rep. Olin "Tiger" Teague, Rep. George Mahon, Senator John Tower, Rep. Jamie Whitten, and dozens more.

At prayer breakfasts near Christmas, I brought the organ to the Capitol so we could sing Christmas hymns. We loaded the organ on a dolly, rolled it down the halls of the Cannon Office Building, through the tunnel under Independence Avenue, and up to the Capitol. The trip took about fifteen minutes, and attracted a lot of attention. Usually, Molly Kellogg was organ wrangler. Once we encountered Vice President Al Gore in the hall and entreated him to sign the organ—which he did, on the spot.

All the members of our Congressional Prayer Breakfast have signed their names on the organ—proof they attended at least once! Years ago, I had to make room for new signatures, so I painted over older names I didn't recognize. Maybe someday archaeologists will scrape the layers of paint and puzzle over the forgotten names.

Omar Khayyam may have written (as translated by Edward Fitzgerald):

The Moving Finger writes; and having writ,
Moves on: nor all your Piety nor Wit
Shall lure it back to cancel half a Line,
Nor all your Tears wash out a Word of it

. . . but *I* say, don't kid yourself! You can cancel out MORE than half a line. I know, because I've done it!

When I retired from Congress and packed up my Washington office, I took my desk and chair, a hundred boxes, thousands of memories—*and* the red pump organ. These days, it sits in my Austin office at Brown McCarroll & Oaks Hartline, which is VERY quiet. But now and then, a plaintive gospel tune floats down the halls, and the busy attorneys stick their heads out of their offices and smile. I'm exercising old bellows—the organ's and mine!

The most recent person to sign the organ was President Bill Clinton, when he spoke in Austin in October 1995 at U.T.'s Liz Carpenter Lectureship. Despite critics from the left and right, the President is right in the middle of the organ—in this case just above the sheet music. As I play, I keep an eye on him.

One of my favorite hymns is "When the Roll Is Called Up Yonder." Members of Congress like that hymn a lot. Perhaps we like to think we'll be there when the roll is called up yonder, too. And I think many will. Despite publicity to the contrary, most members of Congress are decent people trying hard to do the right thing. I know these people, and I love them.

When the roll is called up yonder, I plan to be there to check them in.

*President Reagan signs the Social Security
Reform Bill, 1983. Although Claude Pepper
and Tip O'Neill initially opposed revamping
Social Security, they were front and center at
its signing, and Jake, who spearheaded reform,
peeks out from the back row.*
LEFT TO RIGHT: *Alan Greenspan,
Rep. Dan Rostenkowski, Senator Bob Dole,
Jake, Rep. Claude Pepper, Rep. Bob Michel,
Senator Daniel Moynihan, Speaker of the
House Tip O'Neill, Rep. Barber Conable,
Vice President George Bush.*

Twenty-five

Preserving
Social Security

Social Security is one of our most precious national assets. But fifteen years ago we came close to losing the entire system. And without careful planning, we run the same risk today.

In 1981, when I was chairman of Ways and Means' Social Security Subcommittee, we warned Congress that the Social Security program was going broke. We were roundly criticized for "scaring the old folks." But we saw the Social Security Trust Fund diminishing and knew a crisis was pending.

We held subcommittee hearings. Jack Svahn, Social Security Commissioner, agreed with our basic findings. Veteran Social Security experts like Bob Ball, former Social Security Commissioner, and Bob Meyers, Assistant Deputy Commissioner, also agreed that something needed to be done.

In the winter of 1981, Treasury Secretary Donald Regan testified before Ways and Means and attempted to explain the trickle-down theories of "Reaganomics." After listening to Secretary Regan's sanguine predictions that all we had to do to get the U.S. economy moving was pump up consumption, I called his explanation "jelly bean talk," my reference to the President's beloved candies. The phrase "jelly bean economics" was seized upon by reporters at the hearing and appeared extensively in the media. Most people understood that Social Security's troubles were dire and required more than a hypothetically pumped-up economy.

Still, Congress wouldn't listen and wouldn't act. It still saw Social Security as a sacred cow that no one could touch.

But the Social Security Subcommittee, headed by professional staffers Bill Kelley, Fred Arner, and Janice Gregory knew the truth: the Social Security program was going broke fast. We fashioned a Social Security bill that offered a clear course of action.

Amenable, affable Tip O'Neill called a steering committee caucus to discuss our bill. My good friend Rep. Claude Pepper (D-Fla.) was against raising the retirement age from sixty-five to sixty-seven. Pepper's opposition, among other reasons, was because German Chancellor Otto von Bismarck had set sixty-five as the official age of retirement in the German empire—a century ago! Although I was exasperated, I could see Pepper's point: he argued that some people's jobs are such hard physical labor, they *must* retire at sixty-five.

In effect, the caucus rehashed the same subjects and argued the same arguments. At the end of the caucus, with no recommendations made and no action taken, Speaker O'Neill asked cheerfully if we had found the meeting helpful!

I told O'Neill and the group what LBJ used to tell us bungling staffers: "*Please* take the rest of the day off. Go home. You've helped me today as much as I can stand!"

Opposition to changing Social Security came from labor, from the Education and Labor Committee, from the House Committee on the Aged (chaired by Representative Pepper), and even from the old Social Security warrior Bob Ball. But our subcommittee was determined. We held further caucuses to acquaint members of Congress with the facts. We told the Social Security Commissioner, President Ronald Reagan, and Speaker O'Neill that we had prepared a bill and intended to pass it out of committee. Still, no word came from the White House. So we said in effect: if you don't make a recommendation for a new Social Security bill, we'll pass *our* bill! It was bold talk, but we knew the system was on the verge of collapse, and we had to have the administration's support. But we didn't get it. We failed to get the bill out of committee by two votes.

In September 1981, President Reagan finally sent his proposal, which was to reduce benefits for early retirees from 80 percent to 55 percent, to reduce spousal primary insurance from 37 percent to 27 percent, to phase out retirement earnings tests, and to reduce the benefits of workers with certain pension plans. Reagan's plan would have made it more difficult to qualify for disability benefits, because a medical determination test was required (previous standards of age, work experience, and education were not taken into account).

Well, the President's proposal hit the fan! The media and national organizations favoring the elderly went after Reagan tooth and toenails. Hastily, Reagan withdrew his proposal on September 24, 1981, in a televised address to the nation, and called for the formation of a fifteen-member bipartisan task force to come up with recommendations. And with that, the Republicans retreated from their tentative first effort at Social Security reform.

However, Speaker O'Neill did agree to President Reagan's call for a bipartisan task force to examine the issue and make recommendations. Luckily, the President appointed Alan Greenspan chairman of the task force. It was one of the smartest things Reagan ever did.

I declined to serve on the commission because I was already serving as Chairman of the House Social Security Subcommittee; I thought I should be neutral and wait for the commission's action. But Social Security Subcommittee members Barber Conable and Bill Archer did serve, and pushed for reform.

Alan Greenspan led the task force in the right direction. He used our 1981 bill as the basis for a bipartisan bill. Yet nothing much was done by the task force in late 1981 or 1982. Months passed without action. Barber Conable and I tried to get things moving in the fall of 1982, but the White House was reluctant to stir things up just before the general election in November.

When the vote came in November, the Republicans were badly trounced: over fifty new members were elected to the House, many of them Democrats. The Social Security issue was given credit for the Republican defeat.

After the first of January 1983, things began to happen. The task force made essential changes, agreeing to extend coverage, tax benefits, and raise rates. Our subcommittee endorsed Greenspan's new proposal in principle and took it to the floor of the House, where it passed in April 1983, just thirty days before a new cost of living adjustment (COLA) was to take effect, and sixty days before the Social Security program would have been unable to pay recipients full benefits.

When that happened, there was praise all around for those of us who "saved Social Security." But it was an emergency operation that saved the patient's life, and at the last minute.

I was proud of my 1981 fellow committee members from both parties: Andy Jacobs (D-Ind.), Dick Gephardt (D-Mo.), Bill Cotter (D-Conn.), Frank Guarini (D-N.J.), Jim Shannon (D-Mass.), Don Bailey (D-Pa.), Phil Crane (R-Ill.), Bill Archer (R-Tex.), Bill Gradison (R-Oh.), and John Rousselot (R-Calif.). In 1983, Bob Matsui (D-Calif.), Wyche Fowler (D-Ga.), Bill Thomas (R-Calif.), and Beryl Anthony (D-Ark.) joined the committee, along with staffers Erwin Hytner, Patricia Dilley, and Chuck Brain. The committee was subjected to intense criticism, yet provided leadership. As much as any group, we have been credited with saving Social Security.

During our floor debate, I pointed to the quotation by Daniel Webster inscribed in the ceiling above the Speaker's podium, and said: "Let us go forth to build up and protect our national resources, that we, too, in our time may do something worthy to be remembered."

I think we did.

COST OF LIVING INCREASES

After the Social Security Reform Bill passed in 1983, funds began to flow into the Social Security Trust Fund, and confidence in the system was restored. Basically, the bill gradually increased the age at which full retirement benefits would be paid from sixty-five for people born before 1935 to sixty-seven for people born in 1962 or after, increased contributions from employee and employer, extended coverage, and taxed benefits.

Over the years, many people have asked me: how did Social Security get into trouble in the first place? A primary reason is legislation Congress passed in 1972–1973, which automatically tied Social Security benefits to the rate of inflation. Congress made the system "dynamic," or "active"—which means we granted annual cost of living adjustments (COLAs). It was the fair and compassionate thing to do.

It isn't right to expect Social Security retirees to live in the 1980s on benefits earned decades before, when salaries, benefits, and expenses were much less. But COLAs have cost the system a bundle. Realistically, that's when Social Security's problems started—when Congress granted COLAs. Some people debate this, but I think that's when the trouble began.

THE GREAT "NOTCH" CONTROVERSY

The flap over COLAs was acrimonious, but it was nothing compared to the controversy over the "Notch"—the disparity which occurred when Congress passed legislation in 1977 that reduced benefits granted to people born after 1916.

As David Koitz, with the Congressional Research Service, pointed out, each cost-of-living adjustment up to that time had raised not only the benefits of people already retired, but the eventual benefits of future retirees as well. Koitz wrote, "In the absence of the 1977 legislation, the system would have paid benefits at some point that exceeded a future worker's final earnings."

Moreover, these faulty COLA rules were contributing to a rapid depletion of the Social Security trust fund. Whereas an average wage earner born in the years 1895–1905 had been eligible for annual Social Security benefits equal to 30–34 percent of his or her final year's earnings, the rate had gone up to 45 percent of the final year's earnings for people born in 1912, who retired in 1977, and was slated to rise to 54.4 percent for those born in 1916, who would retire in 1981.

In 1977—in a move designed to improve the system's solvency—Congress passed legislation that reduced benefits that would have been paid to people born on January 1, 1917, and after. People born before that date would receive benefits based on the previous law. Those born after January 1, 1917, would experience a gradual reduction in benefits. This reduction was phased in over a five-year period, for people born in the years 1917 through 1922. For instance, upon retirement, an average wage earner born in 1917 would receive annual benefits equal to 49 percent of his or her final year's earnings. People born in 1918 would receive 46 percent; those born in 1920, 41 percent. The rate for those born in 1921 and afterward would be around 41–43 percent.

January 1, 1917, was an arbitrary date, but like any deadline, it caused problems. For instance, consider two retired automobile workers, one born December 31, 1916, the other born January 1, 1917. Even though both workers might have been employed at the same automotive plant, drawing the same salaries, and born just twenty-four hours apart, the "older" retiree might receive as much as $110 a month more than his "younger" coworker.

However, Congress had to choose a specific date to change the system; the line had to be drawn somewhere. It was hoped that by phasing in the change over a five-year period, we would make it possible for people to adjust without undue financial hardship. We wanted to avoid a "cliff"—an abrupt, drastic reduction of benefits.

That five-year phase-in, designed to give retirees time to adjust, became known as the "Notch," and people born in 1917–1921 became known as "Notch babies." Notch legislation was designed to be fair and helpful and, in general, it was. But national organizations like the Committee to Preserve Social Security and Medicare, headed by Martha McSteen, a previous acting Social Security Commissioner—and someone who should have known better—saw it differently, and started an all-out campaign to "correct" the law. A few other organizations joined McSteen's group. Notable exceptions were the American Association of Retired Persons, the AFL-CIO, the National Association of Municipal Employees, and the National Taxpayer's Union. They knew changing the law was a mistake. It was estimated that revoking the Notch and not correcting the overgenerous law could cost the Social Security System as much as $200–$300 billion by the year 2020.

By 1980 I was Chairman of the Social Security Subcommittee. I began to receive letters by the thousands demanding we correct the "unfairness" of the 1977 legislation. Town meetings were held throughout the country, and members of Congress were besieged to change the law. Over the next few years, hundreds of members of Congress signed up to repeal the 1977 legislation. It was almost a stampede.

As chairman, I knew that our subcommittee had tried to help, not hurt, Notch retirees. Social Security couldn't help anybody if the system went broke. All Notch year babies were receiving more benefits than future retirees! Notch babies hadn't been hurt; they just weren't getting as much as pre-Notch recipients.

For Social Security to return to the pre-1977 system would have cost $30–60 billion *per year*. Members of Congress who caved in to interest groups urged us to "take it out of the Trust Fund." I couldn't accept this proposal. My subcommittee held the line, and over the next few years, the Reagan, Bush, and Clinton administrations agreed.

I like to think that my subcommittee was in part responsible for defeating the Notch question. I urged members not to sponsor Notch legislation, and I spoke out against changes. It was a tough time, but it would have been irresponsible for us to succumb to pressure.

The House of Representatives never allowed Notch legislation to come to the floor for a vote, but in 1992 the Senate did, when Senator Terry Sanford (D-N.C.) tried to slip his Notch legislation into an appropriations bill. That motion failed by the narrowest of margins: 49 to 49, when Senator Lloyd Bentsen objected that Sanford's amendment violated the Social Security "firewall." The firewall provision requires that if Social Security benefits *are* increased, there must be new revenue to pay for it. The firewall is the security that holds the system in place.

Finally, the House and Senate agreed to establish a national commission to study the Notch issue. The commission issued its report in December 1994, concluding that "benefits paid to those in the Notch years are equitable, and no remedial legislation is in order." The report also observed of those retirees born just before the Notch years (before 1917), who had been grandfathered into the plan: "in retrospect, Congress *probably* should have limited the benefits of those who were grandfathered." But in 1994, it was fifteen years too late; to do so then would have been a hardship on people who had already reached the age of seventy-five or more.

Thus ended the Notch saga. My only regret is that we *probably* shouldn't have grandfathered those born before 1917. But that's hindsight now.

Most of all, I'm proud that our subcommittee refused to buckle.

Subcommittee chairmen who succeeded me—Andy Jacobs and the current Social Security Subcommittee Chairman, Jim Bunning—have held the line, as well. As Chairman Bunning said, there's been too much "demagoging for dollars."

I have been given a lot of the credit for stopping the Notch legislation. Rep. Dick Durbin (D-Ill.) liked to call me "the father of the Notch."

CONGRESS MUST PROTECT AND PRESERVE SOCIAL SECURITY—NOW!

Since the enactment of the 1983 Social Security Reform Bill, Social Security has become the most effective—and popular—entitlement program in the U.S. government. It's the granddaddy, the flagship of all entitlement programs.

Social Security's active COLAs have kept pace with inflation. We should remember that the Trust Fund is still in good shape. In fact, Social Security couldn't go broke within five years *even if we abandoned nearly all controls.*

However, storm clouds are gathering. The Social Security Trustees in mid-1995 starkly pointed out that Social Security's annual deficit is 2.17 percent—and growing. This isn't speculation, rumor, or political pontificating. Based on a seventy-five-year projection, the Trust Fund needs an immediate infusion of $60 billion—or more—paid annually for seventy-five years in order to say it is solvent.

If we don't make corrections now, the program could be in peril as soon as the year 2010. This deficit *must* be corrected. Otherwise it will only get worse. Nobody can correct it but Congress.

Unfortunately, both political parties have closed their minds to changes, unless the public understands the gravity of the situation and demands that changes be made. The truth is that our growing Social Security deficit can be slowed and eventually halted by phasing in changes—*not* by waiting to the day of reckoning to suddenly raise taxes.

Politically, Social Security is everybody's hot potato. The Republicans are scared to death of Social Security. They got burned in 1982, so they'll put off even debating it until after the 1996 general election. But the Democrats are afraid of Social Security too. They'd rather make the Republicans the bad guy by forcing them to act first. The Democrats would like people to think they'll *never* make changes or take away benefits.

Both sides are wrong. If we don't begin debating Social Security until 1997, changes won't take effect for four to six years. By that time Social Security's projected annual deficit could be as large as $100 billion.

As former Chairman of the House Ways and Means Social Security Subcommittee, on September 27, 1994, shortly before my retirement from Congress, I introduced H.R. 4275 "to improve the long-term solvency of the Social Security Trust Fund." Briefly, here's what my bill recommended:

- Gradually, increase the retirement age to seventy. In 1983, we raised the age of retirement from age sixty-five to sixty-seven, effective 2000. People are living longer; we should expect them to work longer.

- Reduce benefits for early retirees. Keep it legal for people to retire early, but enact an additional, reasonable penalty if they do.

- Repeal further increases in Delayed Retirement credit beyond 4.5 percent annually. That's a bonus we can tone down.

- Permanently establish age sixty-five as the conversion age for Disability. *This is important!* Disability today is the fastest rising cost to the Social Security Program. And it is being blatantly abused. People are trying to get retirement based on disability instead of regular Social Security benefits. People have no right just before they retire to suddenly claim disability in order to grab larger benefits than other retirees. If we don't control the Disability system, it will bring down the entire system. Disability is bleeding us.

- Phase in a reduction of spousal benefits to one-third of PIA (Primary Insurance Amount, the recommended formula for reimbursement), instead of the present one-half of benefits.

- Cover state and local employees hired after 1996. This will hurt a few states, but it is inevitable. And it's fair.

+ Cost of living adjustments should be granted every other year, instead
of annually. Recipients need inflation protection, but there's nothing
sacred about *annual* increases. We should look at placing a cap on
COLAs, too.

My suggestions were not acted upon, and the issue remained unre-
solved. But I was determined to have my say before I left Congress. I
wanted it on the record.

It is unfair to promise people that Social Security will, in its present
form, go on forever. If we take that approach, Social Security is headed
for disaster. But if we phase in changes now, they won't affect current
recipients over fifty years of age, and we'll give our young workers time
to plan for retirement. And Social Security will *be* there when they
reach retirement.

In late 1995, some members of Congress suggested "some changes,
usually minor in nature" to the Social Security program. Senator Pat
Moynihan (D-N.Y.) suggested a lesser cost of living increase—reducing
the COLA by one percentage point annually. Moynihan made headlines
for "his bold suggestion." Many newspapers ran editorials of support.

Some changes along those lines must be made. If we take steps now,
we won't cut benefits for current retirees, and we won't have to raise
taxes. But in fact, Congress must make more changes than just a reduction or hiatus in COLAs. It must make the broader changes I have
suggested. There really *is* no other way.

Officials like former Senator Warren Rudman and former Treasury
Secretary Pete Peterson have suggested we apply a "needs test" to Social
Security—give benefits only to people who need the money.

That would be a great mistake. Social Security has been a success
exactly because it has *not* been need tested. It's a great equalizer. How
can we require people to pay Social Security taxes all their working
lives and then, at the end of their careers, tell them they can't draw
benefits unless they prove financial need? The workers of today pay, as
their predecessors did, into the system, in the belief that the money will
be in the Trust Fund when their time comes.

Other officials toy with the idea that we could "privatize" Social
Security—allow a small portion of a worker's Social Security fund

to be invested in stocks or bonds. Investor experts, columnists, and economists inevitably point out that privatizing the system could earn workers more money in their lifetime than Social Security could do. Perhaps, in some cases. There is already an outcry to copy new programs in Chile and other Latin American countries, which offer savings "options."

However, that type of plan doesn't protect the average or low-income worker. And investment in stocks and bonds is always risky. As U.T. Coach Darrell Royal used to say about passing in a football game, "Three things can happen, and two of them are bad." We need to encourage more savings programs like IRAs and 401(k)s, but the basic Social Security system must be kept. Rather than privatizing the system, I would prefer to see the Social Security Committee pass a bill to cure our present Social Security deficit first. We should correct the deficit—saving billions—and *then* talk about new options. However, I realize that the Social Security Committee wants to restore public confidence (especially that of young workers, who think Social Security won't be around when they're ready for it) in the Social Security program.

We must remember that Social Security is not a retirement program. It was never intended to provide people with all the money they need for retirement. It's a *supplemental benefit program*, one which makes sure all wage earners have a "nest egg."

When the United States entered into the Depression in 1929, many people were caught with no economic safety net whatsoever. Congress set out to remedy that situation. The Social Security program which was established in 1935 has been the most successful socioeconomic program in American history. Before we try to convert it into a grand 401(k) or IRA, or some other enticing savings system, we ought to correct the minor weaknesses of our present system.

I'm glad to see writers like Jessica Mathews (*Washington Post*, January 10, 1996) point out that we face a more immediate crisis with Social Security than balancing the federal budget. Mathews cites the growing inequity between the number of retirees and the number of wage earners, calling it "a generational train wreck that is coming."

And yet, if we make changes in the system now, we can save billions of dollars. I hope the public is informed about this crisis, and aware of our alternatives.

Whatever is done, I hope Congress doesn't rely on piecemeal changes. We must take a long-term approach. It's up to Congress to tackle the problem now, and quit pontificating that Social Security must be "off the table."

Social Security is already on every working person's food table, and we must keep it there.

Twenty-six

Who Are You?

Every time I hear about the vanity of politicians, I remember one of my own lessons in humility.

Every politician loves to be called by his or her full title, and recognized as such. It's one of the glories of the job. Even after thirty-one years in office, I never tired of the words "Congressman J. J. 'Jake' Pickle."

In the early 1980s my Washington office was visited by a group of elementary school children from Round Rock, Texas. In advance, their teacher extracted a promise from Molly Shulman Kellogg, my executive assistant, that I would pose for a photo with them in the Capitol Rotunda. I agreed, provided my Ways and Means Committee had finished marking up a bill currently under consideration.

Sure enough, the day of the visit Ways and Means went overtime. Molly kept calling me in committee, gently reminding me that the kids and their teacher were waiting. Finally, after about the fourth call, I admonished Molly, "Don't call me any more. As soon as I get finished, I'll get over there as fast as I can."

Finally, Ways and Means adjourned and I headed for my office, where I was met by Molly and John Bender, my administrative assistant. The three of us raced for the Capitol. "Congressman," Molly said, "the kids are already arranged for the photograph."

"For Heaven's sake, Molly," I said, "Why didn't you suggest these kids have their picture taken with (Congressmen) Marvin Leath or Bill Patman? Round Rock isn't even in my District anymore!"

"Oh, I did, Congressman, but they only wanted you," said Molly.

Oh. Well. Of course. I cleared my throat.

When we got to the Rotunda the kids were arranged in concentric circles, the tallest standing in the back and the smallest sitting on the floor. There were about thirty children. As I approached, before God and everybody in the Rotunda, the children burst into loud applause. The sound ricocheted off the marble and echoed through the Rotunda like thunder. I was very impressed, and felt moved to make a speech.

I spoke about how Alexander Hamilton said, "Here, sir, serve the people governed." And about how John Quincy Adams, who knew that at certain points in the Rotunda sound traveled perfectly, used to lay his head on his desk, feigning sleep so that he could eavesdrop on his antagonists. And here Abraham Lincoln had served briefly in the House before being elected President.

I went on in similar manner for some time, extolling our government and my familiarity with it. Finally I stopped and said, "Well, I've been doing all the talking. I realize that this is the first time many of you have been to Washington, or inside our nation's Capitol. Is there anything you'd like to ask *me*?"

One little girl in the first row quickly raised her hand.

"Yes?" I said.

"And who are you?" she asked.

I couldn't even answer because Molly and John were laughing so hard—Molly trying to cover her face, and John hiding behind a marble column. The Congressman had got his comeuppance!

After that, I always tried to remember "who I am" and where I came from.

Jake and his dog Rex, Big Spring, 1921.

A Little Campus poker game, 1932 or 1933. LEFT TO RIGHT: *Jake, Rick Koberg, John Horany, J. Hubert Lee. "We're playing for matches because nobody had any money."*

Jake, wearing his U.T. swim team letter, on a visit home to Big Spring, 1934. LEFT TO RIGHT: *Janice Pickle Harris, Jimmy Harris, Jake, Judith Pickle, Joe Pickle, Pop, and Mom.*

The University of Texas swim team, circa 1934. Coach C. J. "Shorty" Alderson, in suit and vest, center. Jake is in back row, third from right. "I weighed 140 pounds dripping wet."

VOTE FOR

Jake Pickle

for

PRESIDENT

of

Students' Association

INDEPENDENT CANDIDATE

One of "barb" Jake Pickle's campaign cards when he ran successfully for U.T. student body president, 1937.

*Lieutenant junior grade Pickle, on leave from
the war in the Pacific, stumps for war bonds
at a rally at House Park, Austin, 1943.*
LEFT TO RIGHT: *Sugar Pickle, Ed Clark,
Jake, unknown, Joe Kilgore.
Photo by Neal Douglass.*

*Jake is sworn in as Texas Employment
Commissioner, January 1961.*
LEFT TO RIGHT: *Peggy Pickle, Beryl, Jake,
Dick McCarroll, Graham McCarroll.*

*KVET co-owner Jake Pickle (in hat) sold
radio spots to David Lamme at Lamme's
Candies, 919 Congress Avenue, Austin,
December 1947. "David bought a lot of
spots—and I bought a lot of pralines."*

*Two newspaper ads and the brochure from
Jake's first campaign for Congress, 1963.*

Jake's first magazine cover, 1964.
Caricature by R. Windy Winn.
Austin artist Winn was a copartner in
Syers-Pickle & Winn, Inc., in the 1950s.

The dedication of the Gary Job Corps in San
Marcos, Texas, 1964. President Johnson and
Congressman Pickle supported the establishment of the Job Corps, but Texas Governor
John Connally didn't. What LBJ is whispering into Jake's ear at the podium is "Wonder if
we can get John to say something positive
about the Job Corps program this morning?"

*President Johnson speaks at the dedication of
Agudas Achim Synagogue, Austin, December
1963. Lady Bird Johnson, lower far left. Beryl
and Jake, directly behind LBJ. Jessie Kellam,
manager of KTBC-TV, to Jake's left.*

Reception for President Jimmy Carter,
the Cannon House Office Building, 1974.
Rep. Bill Burleson is to Jake's left;
Rep. John Murphey to Jake's right.

Jake performs with the Ballet Folklórico Atzlán de Tejas at Austin's Fiesta Gardens, September 1980.

PART FOUR

THE
CAMPAIGN
TRAIL

Twenty-seven

"G"
as in Jesus

In 1932, former Governor of Texas Miriam "Ma" Ferguson was trying for a comeback, running against incumbent Governor Ross Sterling.

Ma's husband, Jim "Pa" Ferguson had preceded his wife as Governor of Texas in 1915–1917. "Ma and Pa" made a great pair. Pa was a great stump speaker in the Populist tradition. Often at Ma's rallies he entertained the crowd, warming them up before his wife, the actual candidate, made her speech. Pa, who called himself "Farmer Jim," was always promising to help the little man. Farmer Jim would say, "I'm going to put the fodder on the ground where the calves can get it."

One of Jim Ferguson's routines, and one much appreciated by Depression-era audiences, was to poke fun at Governor Sterling, who before his election had been a wealthy Houston oil man. Farmer Jim joked that despite Sterling's highfalutin' airs, the Governor was still nothing more than oil field trash, too country to be governor.

To illustrate that you can't make a silk purse out of a sow's ear, Pa often told the following story at Ma's campaign appearances. It never failed to bring down the house. One day, young state representative Herman Jones from Decatur was in Ferguson's audience. Courtesy of Herman Jones, here is Jim Ferguson's classic campaign story:

Governor Sterling had been invited to a deer hunt on the Anacacho Ranch near Uvalde. He went to the ranch directly from a speaking engagement and inadvertently left his deer rifle in his office at the State Capitol.

When he discovered the error, he called his administrative assistant, Pat Daugherty, long distance to make sure Daugherty found the rifle and brought it to the ranch. But when Sterling placed the call, there was so much static on the rural line that he and Daugherty could hardly hear each other.

Sterling kept saying, "Pat, this is the Governor. *The Governor!* When you come to the ranch tomorrow, bring my gun. It's at the Capitol."

And Daugherty would say, "What? What? Who is this?"

Exasperated, Sterling would repeat the request, talking slowly and loudly into the receiver, but Daugherty could hear only part of what he was saying. Over and over, Daugherty would say, "Hello! We have a bad connection. What do you want?"

Finally Sterling became exasperated and—according to Ferguson—reverted to his old, country self. He lost his temper and shouted, "Pat, now you listen to me! And write this down! This is the GOVERNOR. When you come to the ranch tomorrow, BRING MY GUN. G-U-N. 'G' as in Jesus, 'U' as in onion, and 'N' as in pneumonia! *Gun*, dammit!"

What's James Buchanan Ever Done for You?

James P. Buchanan represented Texas' Tenth Congressional District from 1913 to 1937. Central Texas' Lake Buchanan and Buchanan Dam are named in his honor. Buchanan's political savvy and his longevity were legendary.

In that slower era before television or multimedia, most political campaigning was done outdoors at parades and rallies. A good rally was considered a fine summer pastime, no hotter than spending the evening sitting on your own porch and a lot more entertaining. It was where you got first-hand information about the candidate, where speakers rolled up their sleeves and displayed their wit.

In the Austin of a half-century and more ago, the traditional spot for rallies was Wooldridge Park. Then and now, Wooldridge Park occupies an entire block on Guadalupe Street, just south of the Travis County Courthouse.

A white-columned grandstand nestles in a deep depression in the center of the park. Around it, the slopes form a natural amphitheater. Today, the grandstand is mostly ornamental, but back then candidates often spoke there while their audience sat on the hillside. People brought blankets, fans, and children and made an event of it. At a good rally, every foot of grass at Wooldridge Park was covered with people.

Austinite Colonel C. N. Avery was at just such a rally in the early

1930s when one of Buchanan's opponents in the grandstand was trying to convince the audience that it was time to replace the Congressman. Colonel Avery and his son Buck told this great political story often.

"What man here can say he has a job for which he can thank James Buchanan?" the opponent bellowed. People looked at each other, but no one responded.

"And who among you has a roof over your head as a direct result of action you know to have been taken by James Buchanan?" Other than a baby's cry, no sound broke the silence.

"In fact," thundered the candidate, "I implore—I demand—that you ask yourself: what's James Buchanan ever done for you? In fact, what has James Buchanan *ever* done?"

Slowly, a man stood in the back row. As people craned their necks, he cupped his hands and yelled down the slope, "I'll tell you what James Buchanan's done!" he cried. "He's beaten every single sumbitch who's ever run against him!"

James Buchanan did it again that year, too.

Love, Bess

Jimmy Allred, Governor of Texas from 1935 to 1939, was a popular governor. Allred, who served between Governors "Ma" Ferguson and W. Lee "Pappy" O'Daniel, brought intelligence and dignity to the Governor's Mansion during an especially flamboyant period in Texas politics. But there was a playful, romantic side to Allred that wasn't as well known. He could be a matchmaker, as one Austin couple learned.

In 1936 the Governor of New Mexico, Clyde Tingley, invited Allred to join him for a campaign tour through New Mexico in behalf of the Roosevelt-Garner presidential ticket. Allred accepted, and invited twenty-five-year-old state representative Herman Jones to accompany him.

Jones was flattered, but he had a problem: he was in love with Bess Harris of Austin. He didn't want to leave Bess for even a few days! However, duty called; Jones knew it was a great opportunity. So Jones made Bess promise to write him a long letter marked "Personal" and mail it in care of General Delivery, Carlsbad, New Mexico. Carlsbad was mid-point in the tour. Jones could look forward to it.

When Allred and Jones reached New Mexico, Governor Tingley had arranged appearances in half a dozen cities. So many people were in the entourage that several cars were necessary to transport everybody from city to city. One morning Tingley announced that there had been a change in plans. Tingley said he had been assured by the mayor and city council of Carlsbad that the city was solidly behind the Roosevelt ticket. So they would skip Carlsbad and go directly to the next city on the tour.

Jones was crestfallen. His disappointment was obvious even to Allred. As the Governors' entourage raced down the highway, Allred asked Jones what was the matter. Jones admitted he had been expecting a letter in Carlsbad from his sweetheart. Allred passed this information on to Tingley, and the two governors conferred.

In mid-route, an order was given. The entire caravan came to a halt on the highway, then reversed direction and raced thirty miles to Carlsbad. The cars stopped in front of the U.S. Post Office, and a happy and expectant Herman Jones ran up the steps to get his letter. But there was no letter! Jones sought out the postmaster, explained the situation, and asked him to look. But no letter could be found.

Bess, busy working in Dallas for the Texas Centennial Commission, had also been traveling with friends in California. She had simply forgotten to write!

When at last the tour was over and Herman Jones and Jimmy Allred were back in Texas, Allred teased Bess about her oversight. Then Allred said, "Bess, you and Herman ought to get married. If you'll leave Dallas and move back to Austin, I'll get you a job. Between what you and Herman make, you can afford to get married."

Bess and Herman thought that was a good idea and did exactly that.

Twenty years later, former Governor Allred, then a federal judge in South Texas, was hearing a case in New Mexico. One day Herman Jones got a postcard postmarked Carlsbad. It said, "Dear Herman, Just checked with General Delivery. That letter's not here *yet*! Love, Jimmy."

When Allred acted as matchmaker, he did the citizens of Travis County a favor, too. Herman Jones served for over twenty years as a much loved and respected Judge of the 53rd District Court, Austin. His and Bess' union lasted fifty-seven years, until Herman's death in 1994.

Thirty

The First Time
I Met Jean

In 1956 Price Daniel was elected Governor of Texas and, along with Daniel, I was swept back into politics full time. By then I had pulled out of Syers-Pickle & Winn, Inc., and was doing public relations on my own, working out of the bedroom of my house. It wasn't much of an office, but I was on the road most of the time anyway. Wherever there was a telephone or a political campaign, there was my office. Austin attorney (later Associate Justice of the Supreme Court of Texas) Joe Greenhill served as Daniel's campaign manager, and I was hired as campaign organizer. It was a hard, bitter fight; we defeated Ralph Yarborough by only four thousand votes. Daniel was sworn into office on January 15, 1957, and after the turmoil of the campaign, things seemed to be settling down to normal.

Of course, "normal" is a relative term. Nothing in politics is ever normal. Every time things were normal, something happened to shake me up.

In 1957, Daniel appointed me Assistant Executive Director of the State Democratic Executive Committee. SDEC offices were in the Austin Savings and Loan building on Lavaca, just across the street from the Governor's Mansion.

Each morning I would clip the newspapers and walk the clippings and other information the Governor needed across the street to the

Mansion. Often, Daniel would call with a question or a problem, and we would have an impromptu meeting. I was literally a stone's throw from the Governor.

Another of my duties as SDEC chairman was to accompany the Governor when he traveled. I was the "wood and water man," which meant I was responsible for all the details. I was the guy who saw that the luggage was on board the plane and made sure that we were running on schedule, that the right dignitaries were on hand to meet the Governor when we arrived, and that our accommodations were acceptable. Our trips were often fast and complicated appearances, but it was a challenge to make sure things ran smoothly, and I enjoyed that.

After the first few months, I felt that the Daniel administration was up and running. I was congratulating myself on how well I was doing. I was making a name for myself in the Texas Democratic Party. I was an advisor to the Governor, with whom I traveled around the state on official business. I didn't have much money, but I had as much politics as I could handle, which was a lot. Life was OK.

That was when the Governor and I had occasion to fly to Houston. When I made the arrangements, I learned that Mrs. Daniel—Jean— would be accompanying us. That was fine with me, because I liked Jean. She was as sweet and even-tempered as she was beautiful.

We arrived at the airport amid our usual last-minute flurry and boarded a small private plane. We were its only passengers. That morning, an editorial in the newspaper had been favorable to Daniel, and it looked as if legislation we supported was headed for passage. As we settled into our seats, I was in an ebullient mood.

"Well, Jake," Daniel commented. "You're certainly in fine spirits this morning."

I looked across the aisle at the Governor and Jean, and thought that, yes, things were going very well indeed. I allowed myself to reminisce a little.

I said, "Governor, I'm just sitting here remembering the first time I met you and Jean."

Daniel smiled and said, "Oh, is that right? When was that?"

I said, "It was back in 1939, when I was NYA Area Director in Palestine. Elizabeth Stafford (Hutchinson) got a group together to spend the weekend at Elkhart Lake outside Palestine. I remember it well, because that's the weekend I met both of you, and I was very impressed."

I noticed that the Governor cleared his throat and looked at me nervously, then tightened his tie. He started to say something, but I plunged ahead.

"I remember thinking that Jean was one of the loveliest women I'd ever met, and that you were a lucky man, Governor, to have won her affection."

Daniel began, "Well now, Jake, I don't think . . ." but Jean leaned forward, her eyes bright. She said, "Please go on, Jake! I want to hear more about that first meeting. Why were you so impressed?"

"Well," I said, warming to the memory, "I was taken by your beauty. And I thought the two of you went together so well—that you made the perfect couple. I've thought about that first meeting many times. And now, almost twenty years later, the three of us are still friends.

"Here you are," I nodded at Daniel, "Governor of Texas. Jean is First Lady, and I'm traveling to Houston with you. It's like old times, so I was just thinking back to the first time I met Jean."

The Governor stammered, "Jake, I believe you're remembering another occasion . . ." at which point Jean burst out laughing. She said, "Jake, that wasn't me in Palestine. That was Kathryn Spence!"

Price Daniel had gone out with another young woman before he met Jean Baldwin, whom he married in 1940.

The Governor blushed and looked down at his lap. I sat back, utterly embarrassed and finally—blessedly—stunned into silence.

The Governor and Mrs. Daniel never let me forget my soliloquy about "the first time I met Jean." Even today whenever there's a lull in the conversation, Jean likes to tease me about how impressed I was by her at our first meeting.

I'm not likely to forget again!

President Harry Truman and candidate for Congress Homer Thornberry campaign aboard "The Harry Truman Special," 1948. Senator Lyndon Johnson is to the left and below the microphone. Photo courtesy of Homer Thornberry.

Thirty-one

Ticket, Please

Federal Judge Homer Thornberry, who served Texas' Tenth Congressional District as its Congressman from 1948 to 1963, learned early in his political career how fleeting is fame.

In 1948, Thornberry had just won the nomination for the Democratic Primary, defeating his friend Creekmore Fath for the Congressional seat just vacated by newly elected Senator Lyndon Johnson. In those days the Democratic nomination was tantamount to winning the election the following November. So when Thornberry became the Democratic Party's candidate, for all purposes his campaign was over.

That fall, President Harry Truman, who was running for re-election, was crisscrossing the country in a railroad car, "The Harry Truman Special." The train was on its way from San Marcos to Austin and was scheduled to travel north to Georgetown. Just before the train was due to arrive in Austin, Thornberry, who had not been asked to participate in the campaign at all, was listening to the radio in his home office when he decided on the spur of the moment that he ought to meet the train and wave at Truman. That way Thornberry could at least say he had greeted his party's nominee for President.

So, without a second thought, he jumped in his car and rushed down to the rail depot at Second and Congress. But when he tried to stoop under the police line, the policeman guarding the train refused to admit him.

After a few minutes, another policeman recognized Thornberry and let him through the line. As the Congressman-elect slipped under the rope, the first policeman said sternly, "Hey, buddy, next time get a ticket!"

Timidly, Thornberry walked to the track and was standing there admiring the train, unnoticed in the crowd, when Speaker of the House Sam Rayburn came out of the car, waved at everybody, and said out loud to nobody in particular, "Well, I've always wondered what Congress Avenue would look like from the President's car this hour of the morning." Then Rayburn disappeared back into the coach.

In a few minutes, Senator-elect Lyndon Johnson came out of the train, spotted Thornberry, and waved for him to come up on the platform and meet the President. Thornberry was horrified. "Oh no, that's not necessary," he said, protesting that he had just come to pay his respects to the President. But Johnson wouldn't take no for an answer and, grabbing Thornberry by the arm, he physically hoisted him into the coach.

After appropriate greetings had been made, Johnson and Rayburn decided that since they were in Thornberry's hometown, *he* should be the one to introduce the President. Said Thornberry later, "This scared me to death! When I wandered down to the train, I sure didn't have in mind introducing the President of the United States."

But Rayburn and Johnson kept telling Thornberry, "All you have to say is 'I have the high honor to present to you the President of the United States.'" Thornberry argued and stammered, but finally convinced himself he could do it. And when the time came, he did.

Everyone told Thornberry he was wonderful, and then they insisted he accompany the train to Georgetown and introduce the President there, as well.

"I was trying to talk my way out of it," said Thornberry, "when the conductor came down the aisle and said, 'Ticket please.' He looked straight at me and said, 'Where's YOUR ticket, sir?'"

Thornberry had to admit shamefacedly that he not only had no ticket, he had left home so suddenly he had no money whatsoever. Johnson said, "Thornberry, don't you even have a dollar?"

"No, Senator," Thornberry said, highly embarrassed.

"Well, hell, I'll loan you a dollar," grumbled Johnson, and he peeled off a bill and handed it to the conductor. So Thornberry was permitted to ride the Harry Truman Special to Georgetown, where he performed the same ceremony of introduction to the same accolades and applause.

Thornberry got off the train in Georgetown, and as the Harry Truman Special pulled out of town and he stood waving on the track, he realized suddenly that he was on foot in a different city, with no arrangements and no money to get back to Austin. Trying to think what to do, he began walking down the street, where he spied Austin Mayor Tom Miller, who told Thornberry that his son Tom Jr. was on his way to Georgetown to pick him up. So Thornberry—fresh from the heady triumph of introducing the President of the United States— *twice*—hitchhiked back to Austin with the Millers.

Said Thornberry afterward, "Since that time I've always tried to remember to have at least a dollar in my pocket."

On the Road
with Fleetwood

When I was elected to Congress in 1963, the Tenth Congressional District consisted of ten counties: Travis, Burnet, Blanco, Hays, Caldwell, Bastrop, Lee, Washington, Burleson, and Williamson. Later, redistricting added parts of six other counties: Colorado, Waller, Wharton, Jackson, Fayette, and Austin.

So for years—until later censuses shrank the district geographically—at times I represented sixteen counties, from Burnet County in the west to Jackson County where it met the Gulf of Mexico.

It was a lot of territory to cover, and we covered most of it by car, in grueling day trips which started before daylight and lasted until midnight.

These sixteen counties were as different from each other as night from day. Thirty years ago there were no faxes or computers, and buying television time was a breathtaking luxury reserved for election campaigns. To keep in touch with your district, you covered it in person. That meant a never-ending round of meetings, parades, barbecues, speeches, and festivals. It was fun, and it was how I got to know my people, but it was hard work.

My first district administrator was Fleetwood Richards. I had lobbied Fleetwood hard to convince him to take the job. He had been reluctant because he had a farm in Lockhart, young children, and a pregnant wife. But I kept after Fleetwood, saying I couldn't do the job without him, adding that he would be the Congressman "on site" whenever I was in Washington. One night, after I camped in his living room until 2 A.M., I wore him down until he accepted.

Fleetwood had to learn the job, but so did I. When Fleetwood and I first hit the road, we ran into a few potholes. One of the most memorable potholes was a disastrous one-day swing in 1964 through Waller and Wharton Counties.

I had set up a meeting in Waller County with prominent citizens to discuss the thorny subject of foreign aid. The farmers of Waller County didn't care much for foreign aid; they were interested in problems close to home. To defuse the hostility aroused by the words "foreign aid," I called it "mutual assistance." But whatever I called it, I had to justify to my rural counties every vote—and every dollar—I cast in its favor.

Jake Umlauf, president of the Bank of Waller, agreed to host a meeting at the bank to discuss mutual assistance. Attorney Oliver Kitzman, Waller County Democratic Chairman Harvey Betts, Judge Odis Tomachefsky, and Gus Mutscher, who would later become Speaker of the Texas House of Representatives, agreed to join us.

At the last minute, Umlauf called to say he'd had to schedule another meeting at the bank; why didn't we just meet at Rose's Café outside Waller? I had a fleeting premonition, but I was new at this and hadn't learned to trust my hunches, so I agreed. On the appointed day, Fleetwood and I ended up at Rose's Café with many of the leading citizens of Waller County.

Immediately upon our arrival, I remembered my premonition. Rose's location on Highway 290 meant good business, but bad acoustics. Trucks thundered down the road and shook the little café to its foundations. You could hear the trucks coming half a mile down 290. As they roared past, conversation ceased.

I was seated at a table facing the group. Fleetwood was seated in the audience between Gus Mutscher and Judge Tomachefsky. The two men continued chatting amiably during my presentation. Mutscher had a habit of humming off-key when he was deep in thought, and Tomachefsky's response to conversation was a repetitive, noncommittal, "Tut-tut-tut-tut . . ." Fleetwood, trying to concentrate on what I was saying, was distracted by the humming and tut-tut-tutting going back and forth across his chest.

In addition, the table at which I was seated was directly in front of a large freezer. Every few minutes Rose, who had on a short waitress dress, would raise the lid of the freezer and disappear head first into it to retrieve food. What didn't disappear into the freezer was hiked up and visible to everyone in the audience. They were transfixed, all right—but it wasn't by me.

Just then a school bus rumbled up and discharged a load of high school kids, fresh from band practice and full of energy. The kids ran inside squealing and pumped the jukebox full of quarters. Soon, Patsy Cline and Johnny Cash were wailing from a speaker directly behind my head.

I glared at Fleetwood, and discovered to my astonishment that although his face was serious and attentive, his feet were tapping time to Patsy and Johnny! Pointedly, I glared at his FEET; he looked down, got the message, and hurried off in search of Rose.

Rose didn't know what to do. The jukebox was full of the kids' quarters, so she couldn't pull the plug, and she didn't know how to disconnect our speaker, either. Defeated, Fleetwood returned to his seat. But my audience was so preoccupied they wouldn't have noticed if I had started reading the Houston phone book. I called Fleetwood up to my table. "I don't care how you do it, but you cut off that damn speaker!" I growled.

So Fleetwood went in search of Rose again. In exasperation, she handed him a pair of pliers and suggested he cut a wire that we could see leading from the floor to the speaker. Fleetwood cut the wire—and nothing happened. But in a few minutes, a telephone repairman appeared with tools and a sputtering walkie-talkie to fix the café's telephone line. It turned out he happened to be taking his coffee break in the room next to us when his dispatcher notified him that Rose's telephone line had suddenly, mysteriously, gone dead.

THAT was the end of our discussion of mutual assistance in Waller!

When the meeting broke up, as frustrated as we were, we couldn't go back to Austin because we had a stop in Egypt, in neighboring Wharton County.

Fleetwood and I had set up a meeting to explain new U.S. Agriculture Department guidelines for water and soil conservation to Wharton rice farmers. The new guidelines were explained in a USDA film. It was an early environmental approach to farming and, for that reason, was viewed with skepticism by farmers. Our goal was to talk up the guidelines and try to get the farmers to look at things differently.

About fifty farmers accepted our invitation. A local businessman donated barbecue. After we ate, I planned to stand up, give a brief presentation, then show the film. But right in the middle of dinner, Fleetwood eased up to me and admitted that he had forgotten to bring it!

So I tried my best to explain what the USDA guidelines were. I swallowed and told the farmers they would have to settle for me, because "the film we were expecting from the USDA hasn't arrived yet." I couldn't bring myself to admit the film was back at my office WHERE WE'D LEFT IT! They didn't seem to mind; farmers are distrustful of government anyway, so no news is good news. But I doubt I inspired anybody to farm differently.

On the way back to Austin, I was fussing and fuming about our abortive day. I lit into Fleetwood, telling him we *had* to do better, that we were PROFESSIONALS; we couldn't afford to keep screwing up. I wouldn't stand for it!

The more I bitched, the quieter Fleetwood got. Finally, I wore myself out and we drove in silence. As the car crested the hill at Garwood overlooking the Colorado River, I looked down on that beautiful view, sighed, and said, "Fleet, I know I've been riding you hard. Sometimes I think if I just had a thousand acres of fine bottom land, they could take this job and shove it!"

Fleetwood snorted and said, "Jake, be careful what you wish. I've got almost a thousand acres of land, and I'm about ready to tell *you* to take this job and shove it!"

We had a good laugh and relaxed. Fleetwood defused the situation and made us realize that one bad day was small potatoes in the big scheme of things. The best thing you could do was laugh and go on.

Incidentally, there was something about Wharton County; I was both jinxed and blessed in Wharton County. The people were supportive of me, but every time we went there, something wacky happened. A few months after we met with the rice farmers, Fleetwood and I were in El Campo for a meeting of the Wharton County Historical Society.

A member of Wharton's prominent Northington family presided over Historic Society meetings, and a good-natured Czech named Lucy was Historical Society secretary. Mr. Northington called the meeting to order, and everyone listened respectfully as Lucy, in her Czech accent, read aloud the minutes of the previous meeting. She concluded: "... the meeting was adjourned by George Washington Northington, the Turd." Everybody shifted in their chairs uneasily, avoiding looking at Mr. Northington. Society member Evelyn Krueger beckoned to Lucy and whispered in her ear. I don't know exactly what Evelyn said, but I imagine it was something like, "Oh, Lucy, you ought not to say that. Try again."

Lucy straightened up, her cheeks red. Carefully she enunciated, "The meeting was adjourned by George. Washington. Northington. *The Three.*"

"And," Lucy concluded triumphantly as the Wharton County Historical Society exploded in guffaws, "that completes the reading of our minutes!" and she sat down.

Thirty-three

Beryl Takes
the Wheel

Kyle, Texas, celebrated its 100th birthday in 1980. The proud little city threw a big party, including a parade and speeches. As Kyle's Congressman, I was invited to ride in the parade and say a few words, but I had a conflict. I had already agreed to ride in a parade in Giddings, sixty miles and four counties away.

Like most politicians, I couldn't bear to miss a parade, so I did the natural thing: I decided to attend both! We made arrangements for a helicopter to pick up Beryl and me in Giddings and fly us to Austin. In Austin we would jump in our car and drive as fast as we could to Kyle.

Obviously, timing was crucial. The whole operation had been planned with military precision. Then—wouldn't you know it?—the parade in Giddings ran late. By the time Beryl and I arrived in Kyle, behind schedule and out of breath, their parade was ready to start. All the parade vehicles were in formation, waiting. I jumped out of our car and looked around. Usually at parades, an official gets a convertible in which to ride. This is preferred, because it lets you see *and* be seen. In my case, it also lets me throw out my trademark Pickle pins and pickle "squeaks." But that day in Kyle, there was no convertible. All the other participants were in their cars, looking at us expectantly.

I turned to my campaign aide, Bill Cunningham, who was in charge of the Kyle arrangements. "Bill," I said, "where's the convertible?"

"Uh, Congressman," Bill said uneasily, "we couldn't get a convertible. All we could get was this pickup."

Sure enough, there was a pickup truck parked near the front of the line. And it was a *big* bruiser—a half-ton, flatbed, working-man's truck with livestock fencing. But it was clean, and hastily we hung "Congressman J. J. 'Jake' Pickle" banners on both sides. A pickup wasn't my first choice, but it would have to do. "Well, where's the driver?" I asked Bill.

"He's *supposed* to be here," said Bill, scanning the crowd with a worried look. "I don't know what's happened to him . . ."

At that moment, the parade marshall hurried up, and it was obvious he meant business. His parade was by-God going to start on time, or else! He blew his whistle and ordered everybody to "Move out!" I jumped up in the truck bed and began opening my bags of plastic pickles. "Bill, you'll have to drive," I told him. "There's no other choice."

"Well, Congressman, I don't know . . ." Bill said. "Maybe we'd better wait a little longer."

The parade marshall blew his whistle again, pointed at us and yelled, "Time to go! Now!"

"Quit arguing with me, Bill," I said. "I didn't come halfway across Texas this morning to be left at the curb. Get in and *drive the truck!*"

Bill didn't look happy, but he got in the pickup and turned the ignition key. With the swiftness of a bronc out of the chute, we lurched forward. The sudden movement knocked me on my ass. I stood up, dusted myself off, and said, "Bill! What the hell!"

Through the back window of the pickup I could see Bill bent over the steering wheel, looking grim. He shifted again, and again the truck lurched forward. Down I went! This time, as I picked my self up, I rapped on the window. Bill turned around, looked at me, and mouthed, "Congressman, I can't drive gear shift!"

I could hardly believe that an able-bodied Texas male could not operate a gear shift. On the other hand, I had ample evidence that he could not.

The parade marshall was circling our pickup, and he was livid. Behind us, the cars were stacked up. The marshall yelled at Bill, "Get in this line—or get out!"

Bill and I stared at each other. Then Beryl got out of the truck and said, "I can drive gear shift. Just let me do it."

And Beryl did. She was raised in Jacksonville, Texas, and learned to drive a gear-shift Chevrolet at the age of twelve. Back then, you had no choice. Gear shift was all there was.

But that day in Kyle it wasn't easy, because Beryl was wearing a dress and high heel shoes suitable for riding in a parade, not driving farm equipment. The wheel was stiff and the gears cranky; every time she shifted or braked, of course, she had to depress the clutch or the truck would die. It was a jerky ride, but down the street we went, Beryl applying clutch, brake, clutch, brake all the way. In the bed of the truck, I held on for dear life with one hand, and with the other hand waved and threw out pickles. Grimly, Beryl laboriously shifted gears and ground down on the clutch. Nobody seemed to recognize her or think it strange that the Congressman's wife was behind the wheel. As usual, I got all the attention. By the time we chugged past Tenorio's Grocery and Lex Word General Store, I could see she was getting tired.

Two hours earlier in Giddings, Beryl had sat beside me in a convertible, tossing out pickles. But she really wasn't comfortable doing that sort of stuff, so I had promised her that when we got to Kyle, she could watch the parade from the reviewing stand. It occurred to me that right about now, pitching pickles from a convertible must look pretty good.

Up front, Bill cringed in the passenger seat. In small towns like Kyle where there aren't a lot of downtown streets, a parade will cover the route two or three times; when you finish, you do it again, seeing your reflection in the same store windows, waving at the same bystanders. That's what we did in Kyle. Finally, after the parade had traveled the route a second time, it came to a stop in front of the speaker's platform. I jumped off the truck bed, ran around to the front, and opened the door to help Beryl out. But she couldn't stand up! The tension of keeping the clutch continuously engaged had caused her leg to cramp.

Bill and I stood, waiting for Beryl's leg to relax. But Mayor James Miller kept calling me, and if there's anything a politician hates worse than missing a parade, it's missing a chance to speak. I was forced to

leave Beryl and Bill in the truck while I ascended the speaker's platform—to applause, accolades, and glory!

I always knew I could count on Beryl in a clutch, but she really
proved it that day.

Bill Cunningham is still one of my best friends and advisors. Nothing has changed, except that since the parade in Kyle, I call him "Clutch
Cunningham."

A LIFETIME
OF FRIENDS

*Richard Critz, with the state's attorneys he worked
with prosecuting the 1924 Burleson flogging case.*
BACK, LEFT TO RIGHT:
*Richard Critz, District Attorney (later Governor
of Texas) Dan Moody, Harry Graves.*
FRONT ROW, LEFT TO RIGHT:
J. F. Taulbee, Will H. Nunn.

Thirty-four

Judge Critz's Story

My father-in-law, Judge Richard Critz, was a gentle man with a gruff exterior. Born in 1878 in Starkville, Mississippi, he came to Texas with his family in a wagon. As a young man, he read for the law with Cheshire and Wilcox in Georgetown while teaching sharecroppers' children to read in a one-room schoolhouse. In 1906, the up-and-coming young attorney was elected Granger City Attorney, and in 1910, Williamson County Judge.

Later, when he was practicing law in Taylor, Judge Critz was one of the attorneys who in 1923–1924 helped Dan Moody prosecute the famous Gossett-Burleson flogging case in Williamson County, the case credited with breaking the Ku Klux Klan in Texas—and propelling Moody into the Governor's Mansion. The Judge wasn't a flashy man; he preferred to work on a thing and let others take the spotlight. To my knowledge, he never held a press conference, although during the Gossett trial he posed with other attorneys for the *Austin American* on the steps of the Williamson County Courthouse—the construction of which he had supervised as County Judge a decade before. In the photograph, he looks directly, stolidly at the camera, his right hand in his pocket, a watch chain crossing his vest. Although I didn't know him at the time, his expression is one I remember well.

In 1927, Governor Moody appointed Judge Critz to the Texas Commission of Appeals, and the Critz family—the Judge and Mrs. Critz, James, Genevieve, Chauncey, and Sugar—moved to Austin. In 1935, Governor Jimmy Allred appointed Judge Critz Associate Justice of the Supreme Court of Texas.

Despite his accomplishments, Judge Critz remained plain spoken and stern. His vocabulary was punctuated with phrases from another century: "over yonder," "I'll be there directly"—and, with resignation, whenever Mrs. Critz decided it was time to go calling—"Them that visits has got to be visited."

Even into his seventies, he wore old-fashioned shirts with stiff, removable collars, and his only concession to informality was removing the jacket of his suit. He earned a reputation for writing thoughtful, well-argued opinions that were the envy of the Supreme Court, as of every court on which he sat. He didn't tolerate "foolishness." His mouth was set in a straight line, his blue eyes direct. People took off their hats, if not literally, at least figuratively, in his presence. What everyone recognized about him immediately was his determination and intelligence. Fewer people knew him well enough to recognize his innate kindness.

Sugar (one of the few people on earth not in awe of him) called him "Daddy," and he adored her. Our daughter, Peggy, called him "PawPaw." But he was never anything but "the Judge" to me. I could not imagine calling him "Richard," and "Dick" was totally out of the question; he wasn't a Dick sort of fellow. "The Judge" was a title that reflected what I felt for him: affection and respect.

As the Judge grew old and retired from the practice of law, he took to sitting on the front porch of the Critz home at 1602 West Lynn Street, smoking, reading, and whittling. Often in the evening, I would join him. We got along fine. He never told me what to do, and he never criticized anything I did. Nor did we argue, although his political philosophy was more conservative than mine. Without money and with indefinite prospects, I had married his favorite child, but he never reproached me for that. When, in August 1942, I had written from Chicago, where I was in naval training, asking for Sugar's hand in marriage, the Judge hand-wrote a letter of consent on Supreme Court stationery. "Jake," he wrote, "I have never desired that my daughters marry for money. All I want is that they marry men who are honorable, and can make a living. I believe you fill both bills."

The Judge remembered his own roots. He understood what it was like to have more dreams than money.

Over a decade later, after Sugar's death from cancer, the Judge and I would sit on the porch and he would reminisce. All his stories started the same way: "Well, sir, I never will forget . . ." he would begin, stopping now and then to flick his cigarette. Of course, I had heard all his stories, but I enjoyed them over and over again, if only for the pleasure of hearing the Judge tell them.

Several of his favorite stories concerned Governor Jimmy Allred. While Allred was governor, often on Sunday afternoons he hosted informal domino games at the Governor's Mansion. Judge Critz loved dominoes and approached the game with all the seriousness and concentration that he brought to law. He would line up his dominoes, drum his tobacco-stained fingers on the table, and blow a tuneless melody through pursed lips while contemplating his next move. If his opponent took too long, the Judge would clear his throat and say in a judicial tone, "*The rules say*, all players must play promptly and without hesitation."

Allred relished watching the Judge, especially when his partner played a calamitous domino. The Judge would thunder, "Good God Almighty! Do you know what you've done?" Sometimes Allred and his cronies deliberately misplayed a domino just to get a rise out of the Judge. I imagine Allred invited the Judge to Sunday dominoes for the same reason I listened to his stories—for the fun of watching the man himself.

When Allred retired from the governorship, he became a federal judge in South Texas. Judge Critz owned a farm outside Robstown, near Corpus Christi. Sometimes he drove to Robstown to attend to farm business.

In 1945, six years after Allred left the Governor's office, he was conducting a trial in Corpus on the same day Judge Critz needed to drive to Robstown. On the spur of the moment, Judge Critz decided to stop at the Federal Courthouse and say hello to Jimmy Allred. When he arrived at the courthouse, he made inquiries and was directed to Allred's courtroom.

Allred was at the bench, presiding over the trial, when Judge Critz slipped unannounced into the back of the courtroom. Allred looked up, spied his old friend, and immediately brought the gavel down, hard. Bang! The courtroom hushed.

"Ladies and gentlemen of the court," Allred said in a loud voice, "we have today the pleasure and the privilege of having in our courtroom one of Texas' great jurists, a man I personally know to be of sterling integrity and a brilliant legal mind. Please allow me to introduce to you my great friend and former colleague, Judge Richard Critz of Austin." Allred banged his gavel again. "I am declaring a fifteen-minute recess so I can visit with Judge Critz."

Everyone in the courtroom turned around and stared. Judge Critz nodded and sank into a chair, flustered by the attention and stunned by the unexpected praise.

At this point in his story, the Judge would stop, tap his cigarette, look out at the dark lawn, and say something—it was the same sentence every time, year after year, whenever he told me this story. He would say in a quiet voice, "Jimmy Allred will always be Lord Chesterfield to me."

Saying that always made the Judge choke up a little. Watching the Judge got me choked up, too. I can still see him sitting there in the twilight—in the twilight of his life, remembering a distinguished career, the respect of friends, and the good times.

Judge Critz will always be Lord Chesterfield to me.

"Governor" Pickle

In 1957 or 1958 Governor Price Daniel and I were in El Paso attending a State Democratic Executive Committee meeting. About that time, the states of Chihuahua and Texas were instigating a program to eradicate the yellow boll weevil. So the Governor was in El Paso to officially give credence to the boll weevil eradication program, as well. Jean Daniel was in El Paso with her husband.

Our party stayed at El Paso's Del Norte Hotel, the finest in town. One night after our meeting, Price and Jean, Hazel and Bob Haynsworth, and I decided to go across the border to Juárez.

The Haynsworths knew a bar in Juárez with a good band and a floor show, and Bob Haynsworth called ahead to speak to the manager. The manager was told that the Governor of Texas would be in our party, and we wished no publicity. The manager said we did him great honor. Absolutamente! He would respect our privacy.

When our group arrived at the bar, we were seated at a big table near the band. Now, Governor Daniel was a Baptist and a teetotaler. Officially, he never drank. But he liked Cokes. Every time we went someplace people would offer Daniel a drink, and he'd always decline, saying, "Well thank you, but I don't drink." People expected this, but always felt they had to offer the Governor a drink anyway.

But sometimes Daniel would add, "I'll take a Coke, though. Jake, why don't you get me a Coke?" And I would—but I'd have the bartender pour a shot of bourbon in it. Daniel never mentioned the bourbon—but he always asked *me* to get his Cokes. It was a little game we played for years, one which allowed Daniel to follow his religion, but enjoy a little socializing with a clear conscience.

However, Coke or no Coke, the last thing Daniel wanted was to be recognized in a bar, even a Mexican bar with no constituents.

Everything went fine for a few minutes. Then the band, which had been playing lively Mexican melodies, suddenly stopped, then executed a drum-roll flourish. The Governor and I looked at each other and thought, "Uh oh." He sank lower in his seat.

Then the bandleader announced into the mike, "We are proud to have with us tonight the Governor of the State of Texas"—another drum roll—"the honorable Price Daniel!" Amid the fanfare, a white spotlight swept the dark bar and came to rest on our table.

Nobody moved. Daniel kept his head down.

Again, the announcer said, "Damas y caballeros, permítanme presentarles el gobernador del estado de Tejas!" Another drum roll and the bright spotlight on our table.

Still no movement from Price.

With the spotlight still on us, a third time the announcer called, "Please! Will the Governor of Texas stand and be recognized?"

Finally Jean leaned over and whispered urgently, "Jake, for goodness sake, will you do it?" And Daniel said, "Jake, I bet you've always wanted to be Governor—here's your chance."

So I got to my feet and grinned and waved to thunderous applause, as the band struck up "The Eyes of Texas." I must admit, I got a *great* reception.

Boll weevils and politicians. We're jus' lookin' for a home.

Thirty-six

Dan's Debut

On Halloween night in 1993, veteran newscaster and public relations executive Neal Spelce hosted a party at his Austin home to which he invited old friends, including Lady Bird Johnson. Officially, the party was to "bay at the moon," and sure enough when the moon rose white and full, we gathered on the patio and howled.

Spelce's guest of honor was CBS anchorman and fellow Texan Dan Rather, who was celebrating his birthday. During the evening, Dan told how he first met Lyndon Johnson. Believe me, it was *not* a formal introduction! With permission from Dan, here is his account.

In 1955, Rather was working for KTRH Radio in Houston. Somewhere Rather heard that Senator Lyndon Johnson was going to host an important party at the LBJ Ranch the following Saturday, and Rather took it to mean that Johnson might make an official announcement, maybe even his run for the presidency. "This was pure conjecture on my part, of course," says Rather, "but I talked the radio station into paying my expenses—no mean feat for a small radio station and a near starving broadcaster."

Rather told the station manager it would be big-time news coverage and promised to report live what was happening at the ranch. Reluctantly, the station agreed. Incidentally, Rather's "expenses" didn't include transportation. He hitchhiked!

When Rather got to the ranch, he circulated among the guests, looking for a lead on a hot political story, but he couldn't find anything at all. No one was confirming Johnson's run for the presidency—at least within that inexperienced reporter's hearing. But Rather had promised to call the station by noon, and time was running out. Finally, just before lunch, he asked one of Johnson's aides if he could use the phone, and the guy pointed down the hall to a telephone in the Senator's office.

When Rather got the station on the line and began to broadcast, he was forced to create a story out of a nonstory. He intoned, "This is Dan Rather live from the LBJ Ranch. A lot of speculation's going on here by important political figures, and while no official word has been given, it appears that Senator Johnson may soon make an announcement of great importance—possibly his candidacy for the presidency of the United States. So far, Johnson has been coy about the question, but he is in high spirits. There is every reason to suspect that he may soon make this long-expected announcement.

"This is Dan Rather reporting live . . ."

Rather felt a heavy hand clamp down on his shoulder. He looked up. "It was LBJ, big as life, glaring down at me! He took the telephone out of my hand and spoke into the receiver. 'I don't know who this fellow is, and I don't give a damn. He doesn't have any authority at all to make this statement. As far as I'm concerned, this guy can go to hell. I'm announcing only one thing, and that is he's getting off my ranch right now.'"

With that, the President put the receiver back on the hook and growled at Rather, "Get the hell out of here."

Rather said, "I was frightened out of my wits! I gathered up my stuff as fast as I could, burst out the office door, and headed down the road on foot."

Rather hadn't gone more than a couple of hundred yards when a car eased up alongside him, and a soothing Southern female voice called out, "Now young man, this is Lady Bird. Don't you pay any attention to what Lyndon said. He didn't mean anything. That's just his way. Now you come on back with me. We'll have supper, and you can get acquainted with Lyndon."

Rather was thunderstruck, and greatly relieved. Happily he got in the car and returned to the ranch with Lady Bird. He did stay for supper, and it was the beginning of a lasting friendship with the Johnsons.

Later, Rather learned that these tirades were typical of the President, who was just as quick to forgive as he was to anger.

"I've always wondered," Rather said, "how many times sweet Lady Bird soothed waters that Lyndon roiled."

Thirty-seven

The 88th Club

For thirty-one years I was a member of "The 88th Club." It was a club that paid no dues, produced no minutes, had no official agenda, and accepted no new members after January 3, 1965, but in it were some of the best friends I ever had.

When a person is elected to the House of Representatives or the Senate, he or she becomes a member of a particular Congress. Not just "the" Congress—"a" Congress. Each Congress consists of two one-year sessions. The first Congress was in 1789; 1996 was the second session of the 104th Congress.

I was sworn into office for the first time on December 24, 1963—the first session of the 88th Congress. When I took office, I was one of about thirty freshmen who became members of the House of Representatives' "88th Club."

Since Congress is based on the seniority system, members sworn into office during the same session share experiences and move through the ranks at approximately the same time, so they develop esprit de corps. It doesn't matter whether you're a Democrat or a Republican. As freshmen, you learn together. In many ways, how your members relate to each other determines the effectiveness of your group. Like the members of a senior class or graduates of military training, you love and are loyal to your group.

The 88th Club elected "Sparky" Matsunaga (D-Hawaii) as our president. Sparky was recommended by fellow 88th Club member Phil Burton (D-Calif.). Burton turned out to be one of the most capable men in Congress, so capable, in fact, that years later he lost the race for Majority Leader of the House to Jim Wright by just one vote. Of course, every Texas Congressman (including me) bragged to Wright that *his* was the vote that made the difference!

Somehow I ended up as Secretary of the 88th Club, and I served in that capacity until my retirement from Congress. My job was to issue invitations and organize entertainment. Molly Kellogg on my staff usually got stuck with the invitations. I discovered that lining up the "entertainment" was easy as pie.

Our freshman year, the 88th Club found a sponsor, a lobbyist who could finance our annual dinner. This sort of thing is out of favor now, sneered at as "influence peddling," but it was common practice thirty years ago. Our sponsor was George Koch, a lobbyist representing Sears Roebuck and Co. George and his wife, Helen, sponsored the 88th Club all those years, even after George left Sears to become president of the American Wholesale Grocers Association.

In the beginning, I think George sponsored us because he was friendly with several members of the 88th Club. But after the first banquet, he continued to sponsor us because he got a kick out of our group. One thing I *do* know: George never asked me for a favor or tried to influence my vote on any issue, and to my knowledge he never tried to influence any other member, either.

And oh, those banquets were fun!

Every year, usually around St. Patrick's Day, the members of the 88th Club and their spouses met for dinner at the City Tavern, a swank private club in old Georgetown which claimed President George Washington as an early member. In honor of the holiday, everyone wore green hats, ties, dresses, shamrocks, and any other Irish greenery we could find. Nobody else's hat was as fine as *my* hat—an emerald green top hat made by Texas Hatters' Manny Gammage.

It was a bipartisan group. Any discussion of politics or issues before Congress was strictly prohibited. But the 88th Club's annual banquet was such an exuberant affair that nobody wanted to discuss issues anyway.

Because the members of the 88th Club were hams. Almost everyone in the club could do something musical or artistic. And everyone enjoyed showing off. I guess you could say that the 88th Club survived for so many years *because we hams wanted to perform!*

There were never any speeches. As soon as we sat down, Sparky Matsunaga warmed up the crowd with a few jokes, and then the program got under way. Over the years, the acts changed, but the evening usually went something like this:

Dick Hanna (D-Calif.), a short, impish Irishman with a BIG voice joined six-feet-six-inches-tall Rogers Morton (R-Md.), later Nixon's Secretary of the Interior, in a duet. Morton towered over Hanna, but their voices blended perfectly.

Then Albert Johnson (R-Pa.) played his mandolin—until (because a little mandolin playing goes a long way) we urged him to quit. Bill Hungate (D-Mo.), later a federal judge, sang "Wayne Hays," a song about the Congressman who was disgraced when it became public knowledge he had hired a staffer for talents other than her secretarial skills. "Wayne Hays" was so popular that we made Hungate sing it every year.

Jim Broyhill (R-N.C.) sang "Carolina Moon" with Charlotte Reid (R-Ill.), a *real* professional, because she had appeared on the nationally famous Breakfast Club radio program. Bob Leggett (D-Calif.) belted out "California, Here We Come" and "I Left My Heart in San Francisco" on his trumpet with such force that the veins in his neck swelled almost as large as his horn!

Sometime during the evening Lionel Van Deerlin (D-Calif.) would be called upon to recite "Casey at the Bat," and oh, how Van Deerlin would gesture, swinging Casey's imaginary bat and shouting "Strike Three!" But for all his dramatics, inevitably he forgot a verse until his wife, Mary Jo, fed him the line. He resumed with increased vigor. We enjoyed Van Deerlin's recitation, but we could hardly *wait* until his goof-ups.

Del Clawson (R-Calif.) was a former professional saxophone player who had had his own orchestra. With his sax, he walked from table to table, serenading the guests with their college or state songs.

And then there was Don Clausen (R-Calif.), who twirled the baton!

He must have been a drum major in college, because he would strut into the room, twirling that baton and tossing it high in the air. Or he would pass it behind his back (and around his fifty-inch waist) and *then* toss it in the air. One year he even put lights on the ends of his baton. When someone turned off the lights in the room: show time!

Clausen was a good baton twirler, but he was portly and out of practice, and when the baton went skyward—especially when the lights were off—nervous laughter rippled through the crowd as people ducked for cover. Clausen's shows were always received with much applause (and relief), especially when they were over and no one had been hit on the head.

I remember Bob McClory (R-Ill.) playing Rachmaninoff on the piano. Sparky Matsunaga and Nancy Horton, the wife of Frank Horton (R-N.Y.) sang a duet of "Blue Hawaii." In the early years, our unofficial photographer was Bob Duncan (D-Ore.). Of Scottish descent, Duncan proudly wore a kilt to 88th Club functions. Martha and Sam Gibbons (D-Fla.) were always on the front row, leading the laughter, as was Bill Green Jr. (D-Pa.). Green (later Mayor of Philadelphia) was the son of Bill Green Sr., whose funeral in Philadelphia Beryl and I had attended the cold, tumultuous day of my swearing-in, so long ago. Small world.

As word of our fame—and talent—spread, each year we had special guests who wanted to watch the show. One year, George Koch brought several members of the Wholesale Grocers Association board of directors. Instead of distinguished members of Congress, they got the Ted Mack Amateur Hour. Later, one board member told Koch he was surprised to find us so "human." The man was a master of tact!

Sometimes our special guests performed themselves. Rep. Dan Akaka (D-Hawaii) sang Hawaiian love songs, and Lindy Boggs (D-La.) sang "Alouette." One year Speaker Tip O'Neill and Rep. Bob Michel (R-Ill.) teamed up like Bing Crosby and Bob Hope with "On the Road to Mandaley."

And of course, toward the end of each evening, I was prevailed upon to bring out my harmonica and play "You Are My Sunshine" and "The Yellow Rose of Texas." We saved the best for the last!

Finally, Claude Pepper (D-Fla.) rose. The room hushed as Pepper raised his glass and led us in a simple toast. "To the 88th!" he'd call in his soft, warm voice. After all the high spirits, it was a moment of great poignancy. By reminding us what it meant to belong to the 88th Club, he was reminding us of the friendships in that room, and of our great democratic government. Pepper made us feel so proud.

Then Bill Hungate led us in our closing song, written by his wife, Dorothy. To the tune of "Love Me Tender," the chorus went:

> *"Eighty-eighth, eighty-eighth*
> *Here's a toast to thee*
> *Banner class, the very best*
> *In our his-to-ry!"*

As the years went by and members retired, were defeated, or died, the 88th Club grew a little smaller every year. But it was a loyal group. Those who could come back, did. Even after three decades, the year I retired from Congress the 88th Club still consisted of about ten original members and their spouses.

What made the 88th Club so special? What made us so famous that we became known on Capitol Hill as the best club in Congress?

It certainly wasn't our talent, although we were happy to inflict it upon each other. It was our camaraderie. We became an extended family and, like family, we overlooked our differences and vanities to work together.

I guess every Congressional club thinks it is the best. A club's purpose is to foster cohesiveness. But I believe in all seriousness that the 88th Club was the most loyal club ever to work together in Congress. When I look at the acrimony and partisanship that dominate relationships between Democrats and Republicans in Congress today, I am heartsick. The members of the 88th Club were frequently, passionately on different sides of an issue, but we respected each other.

And who knows? Maybe *because* the 88th Club laughed with (and at) each other one day in March for thirty-one years, we were harmonious the other 364 days of the year.

Thirty-eight

Good-bye to LBJ and Big John

Two men, more than any others, affected my political career: John Connally and Lyndon Johnson. I was privileged to deliver eulogies for both men, twenty years apart.

I heard about LBJ's death at an evening reception on Capitol Hill hosted by Congressman Wright Patman to celebrate the opening of the first session of the 93rd Congress on January 22, 1973. As word spread through the largely Texas crowd, Beryl and I hurried downstairs to my office in the Cannon Office Building and turned on the television. As I listened to the news bulletins on every station, I was saddened beyond acceptance. Although I knew the President had been gravely ill, it seemed impossible that this strong man could really die.

What I regretted most was that LBJ died not at the peak of his career, but in retirement caused by failing health and the controversy over the Vietnam War. I knew the specter of Vietnam would forever influence history's perception of Johnson's presidency, a presidency which had passed more social legislation than any other. I wondered how people would remember LBJ.

That's what I was thinking as images of Johnson flickered across the television screen: how unfair it was, and how people would remember him.

The phone rang in our Washington apartment early the next morning. It was Tom Johnson, who worked for KTBC-TV (and who is currently President of CNN, Atlanta) calling from Austin. He told me that Johnson's funeral service would be held in Washington two days later. Then he added, "The family has requested that you deliver the eulogy." Tom also said that former Secretary of State Dean Rusk was being asked to give another eulogy as a Johnson administration spokesman. But mine would be the eulogy of a friend.

My first reaction was total shock. I knew immediately that this would be no small undertaking. The eulogy would be delivered in the Capitol Rotunda. Via television, I knew the nation—and the world—would be watching.

My second reaction was "I can't do it." However, I knew there was no way I could tell Lady Bird no, and no way I could live with myself if I didn't do it. So I tried to ignore my fear and get to work. The pressure was on. Johnson hated to see a thing done poorly. I could not do *this* thing poorly.

When I arrived at my office I gathered my staff, including my administrative assistant, Tony Profitt, and we began drafting a speech. Over the next twenty-four hours I called old friends, asking for ideas. Margaret Meyer, a former *Dallas Times-Herald* correspondent and a great friend of the Johnsons, called with a suggestion. Margaret recalled one of Johnson's favorite phrases, something his father, Sam Johnson, had often said, and which reflected both men's fierce love for the Texas Hill Country. I made a mental note to use it, and thanked Margaret.

Later that day, I got a call from Jack Valenti, saying that Joe Califano, a former aide to Johnson (and later Secretary of Health, Education, and Welfare) was available to help with copy. I was enormously relieved. Califano came over and joined Profitt and me as we worked on the speech.

I had already written a preliminary eulogy about Johnson the statesman. Profitt and Califano thought that despite the grandeur of the situation, I should take a more personal approach. My remarks listed the biographical details of Johnson's life, which they felt everybody knew. Instead, they suggested I evaluate Johnson's presidency and share my feelings about Johnson the man. I thought that was good advice. So Califano and Profitt huddled at Profitt's desk in the back of the office, where it was quieter. I tried to carry on Congressional business in my office, ducking back to Profitt's desk every few minutes with something I thought should be added. We must have written fifteen drafts—and this was before computers, when each draft was retyped from scratch, with carbons. Claudia Graef Zacharino and Molly Shulman Kellogg typed the speech over and over without complaint.

Finally, at 9 or 10 o'clock the night before the service, I was so exhausted they told me to go home and get some rest. I hadn't been sleeping, I was still in a state of shock about Johnson, and I was worried about giving the eulogy. They convinced me that the best eulogy in the world would fall flat if I was so tired I delivered it poorly. So I went home and they stayed at the office, rewriting. That night I got some sleep, and the next morning I felt better. When I dressed, I put on my "LBJ Air Force One" tie clasp, and I thought, "Well, this is it."

I think I delivered the eulogy on January 24, 1973, all right. I was mindful that my West Texas drawl might sound corny to my international audience. But I spoke from the heart. I said, "As a young man, he experienced poverty and witnessed discrimination. He learned first hand about drought and parched earth, about stomachs that weren't full and sores that weren't healed. He brought water and electricity and housing to the Congressional District which he served. As Congressman, he knew what it was like to be a poor farmer, a working man without a job, a Black, or a Mexican-American, and he set about changing life among his constituents." I knew these things to be true because I had heard Johnson talk about them, and had witnessed some of them myself.

In sixty years in public life I have given many speeches, but none as difficult as my eulogy for Lyndon Johnson. I was afraid I would break down; I was afraid I wouldn't say the right thing. But I did fine until I got to the end, to the line Margaret Meyer had suggested, and then I choked up. The line was ". . . the President will rest in his beloved Hill Country, where . . . his Daddy before him said he wanted to come home. To come home 'where folks know when you're sick, and care when you die.'"

After I finished, the President's aide, whom everybody called Sarge, laid his head on Beryl's shoulder and sobbed. I felt like doing the same thing.

And I remembered the President's last public appearance a few weeks before, when he delivered a speech to a civil rights symposium at the recently dedicated LBJ Library in Austin. He arrived late and walked slowly to the podium. Those of us in the audience noticed that he paused during his remarks, took a pill from his pocket, and swallowed it. When he finished the speech, he was escorted to a large reception room immediately behind the stage, to rest. I found him sitting there, alone. I pulled up a chair. He opened his eyes and said softly, "Jake, I didn't see you in the audience. I should have mentioned your 1964 vote on Civil Rights."

Then he paused. "You know, Jake," he continued quietly, "you've always been there. Some of the others get angry or they leave. But you never have. Lady Bird and I want to do something special for you. And I have something in mind."

We talked quietly a few minutes until he was helped to his limousine by Secret Service Agents. It was the last time I saw him alive.

I don't know if the honor of giving his eulogy in the Rotunda of the United States Capitol was what Johnson had in mind, and I'll never know. I do know that it was more special to me than my words that day could express.

That night, Lyndon Johnson, thirty-sixth President of the United States, lay in state in the Capitol Rotunda. Family and friends took turns standing guard beside his bier as the public came to say good-bye. Beryl and I stood together for about an hour at one end of the President's casket. Secretary of Commerce C. R. Smith of Austin stood at the other end.

In that vast and vaulted place, the only sounds were muffled footsteps on marble and low coughs as hundreds of people filed slowly past the bier. I recognized some of the faces. Everyone was bundled against the Washington winter. Many people were crying. Every face looked pinched and solemn.

As I stood in that magnificent silence, I had time to reflect. I thought about Johnson's remarkable accomplishments, how much the nation owed him, and how much I owed him personally. And I thought about my last conversation with Johnson at the LBJ Library. In response to my silent, unanswered questions the night of Johnson's death, I looked at his casket and assured him: we do care, Mr. President, and we *will* remember.

John Connally's death in June 1993 rocked me as much as Johnson's. While Johnson had always been a towering figure, Connally was my contemporary. He was like me, only better looking!

We had known each other since we were not much more than boys, as classmates and fraternity brothers at the University of Texas. We entered politics together when we became involved in races for U.T. student body president. It was John Connally, working for then-Congressman Lyndon Johnson, who called me one day in 1939 to ask if I wanted to move to Austin to serve as area director for the National Youth Administration. *Did* I! The NYA district mirrored the Tenth Congressional District, so because of Connally, I became Johnson's eyes and ears back home. John's and my personal lives were entwined, as well, since our wives were friends.

The call about John's death came from George Christian. Several times during the last few days, Nellie had told me John's doctors felt that his illness—pneumonia and complications from pulmonary fibrosis—was fatal. Still, we hoped he had weeks to live. When the end came, it was so fast I hadn't absorbed it. Although John had died in Houston, his funeral would be in Austin's First United Methodist Church. Nellie and the family wanted me to give a eulogy.

I agreed to do it, but when I sat down to put thoughts on paper, I faced a decision similar to the one I had faced with Johnson, twenty years before. Should I eulogize Connally the statesman, or Connally my friend?

I decided to eulogize the John Connally *I* knew, not the public figure. I had known John too long and too well to do anything else. This time, I wrote the copy myself. Paul Hilgers and Eddie Reeves in my Austin office made suggestions and, as when LBJ died, I asked friends and family for things they remembered about John. I liked former Speaker of the House Jim Wright's suggestion, Mark Anthony's line from *Julius Caesar*: ". . . that Nature might stand up / And say to all the world, 'This was a man'" and penciled it into my conclusion. John would have enjoyed being compared to "the noblest Roman of them all."

When, the day of John's funeral, June 17, 1993, I climbed to the altar of that venerable church and began, "Old Texas friends have the right to talk, to brag, and to remember what they *want* to remember, and I do so now with pride and love for John Connally," laughter rippled through the church, and I knew it was going to be okay.

I reminisced about how at the university we called him Big John, because he was almost bigger than life—in height, dreams, style, and ego. Law school classmate and later Congressman Joe Kilgore and I called John "the Profile," because his face was as handsomely chiseled as a Roman coin.

I talked about how when he made his mind up, he set that square jaw as firmly as a bulldog. When John ran for Governor against Price Daniel in 1962, I reminded John that because Price had appointed me to the Texas Employment Commission I was honor bound to support Price's candidacy, and John forgave me. Long before John became a Republican I could see it coming, and tried my best to talk him out of it, yet I understood his reasons and forgave him. Despite our political differences, we remained friends for almost sixty years.

There were a lot of memories with me at First United Methodist Church the day we buried John. I had stood at that same altar as John's best man when he married Idanell Brill in 1940. Two years later, I had married Sugar at the same altar, and after Sugar's death in 1952, married Beryl Bolton McCarroll in 1960 in the adjacent chapel. Our family still worships there today.

It was as though John and I had come full circle. My circle is not yet complete, and I didn't want to let John go. It is hard to accept that my friends are leaving me, when there is still so much work to do.

With affection, I talked about John's strengths and weaknesses. I banished grief or regret for what might have been. If Lyndon Johnson's eulogy was the hardest speech I ever gave, John Connally's eulogy came easy. I knew him so well, the surroundings were so familiar, and my memories so sharp, it just seemed natural. Maybe after a half-century of John's and my heated debates, I was eager to have the last word!

The huge church was full. People stood shoulder to shoulder in the vestibule and spilled down the front steps to the street; a hundred others watched the service on closed-circuit television in the chapel. As I

216

surveyed the audience, I found a few unexpected faces. In one pew was former President Richard Nixon, who arrived late and was incongruously seated next to Texas Governor Ann Richards. Later, Governor Richards told me that after they had exchanged greetings, Nixon looked up and saw me in the pulpit. Startled, he whispered to Governor Richards, "Why, that's Jake Pickle! What's *he* doing there?" and the Governor told him I was going to deliver a eulogy.

Later I learned that Nixon had flown from New Jersey, where he was keeping vigil at the deathbed of his wife, Pat. The day after Connally's funeral, just hours before Pat died, Nixon wrote me a note commending me on the eulogy. He even recalled our attending the Arkansas-Texas national championship football game twenty-four years earlier.

Nixon was a hard man, but he was loyal to his friends. He remembered that during and after Watergate, when many people shunned him, Connally never did. They remained friends to the end. Because of the compassionate example of Connally and others, Nixon developed the habit of contacting people he knew to be experiencing hardship and offering his support. And he never forgot those who didn't forget him.

I was not a Richard Nixon fan. Had his impeachment come to a vote in the House of Representatives, I would have voted to impeach him. However, his loyalty to John Connally showed me a side of Richard Nixon I had never known existed. Sometimes a man's suffering makes him more sensitive to others.

I gave one of three eulogies at John Connally's funeral. Lady Bird and John B. Connally III—John and Nellie's grown-up "Johnnie B"— gave the other two. We were followed by the Reverend Dr. Billy Graham, who delivered the sermon. When I spoke, I didn't try to preach or be religious. I left God to the preacher, since I knew he would do a better job than I. After the service, Dr. Graham told me, "Jake, I'm sorry we didn't get to visit, but I'll write," and he did.

I received more compliments on Connally's eulogy than any other speech I've ever given. I don't know whether that reflected its quality or the number of people who watched it live on television, and when it was rebroadcast. I do know my eulogy was interrupted often by laughter; when I finished, people stood and applauded. That had never happened to me before—in a church! As I gathered my notes and prepared to leave the lectern, I looked out and saw relaxed, smiling faces, and I thought maybe I had accomplished what I had set out to do.

After the service, we buried John at the State Cemetery in Austin. He rests under magnificent old oak trees, on a gentle hill overlooking the headstones of Texas heroes. In death—as he preferred in life—he is in illustrious company!

At the conclusion of the interment service, I paused before John's casket for a minute, fingering the floral sprays. Beryl stood behind me. Going home in the car, she said, "You put a Pickle pin in there, didn't you?" and I admitted I did. "The minute you put your hands in those flowers," Beryl said, "I *knew* what you were doing!"

So John went down to his eternal rest with a green Pickle pin atop his casket. I'm sure Nellie understands. Eternity is a long time to spend without the company of friends.

Thirty-nine

Family Talent

In my thirty-one years in Congress, almost every member of my family has endured a variety of activities and discomforts related to having a politician in the house. My son-in-law Don Cook jokingly calls this "the shameless exploitation of the family."

It started early, over fifty years ago, when I was married to Sugar. Sugar had been raised in a political family; she was politically minded. She was also outgoing and funny, so many Austin people who didn't know me from Adam invited me places just to see *her*. Sugar never lived to see me elected to Congress, but she was there at the beginning, when we talked politics with John and Nellie Connally, when I worked for the NYA, as we struggled to get KVET and Syers-Pickle & Winn started, and when I began crisscrossing Texas with Lyndon Johnson. She was assertive and smart. I don't think there was anything on earth she was afraid of, including, when the end came—on January 25, 1952— death. Sugar lived during a time when women didn't run for office; they supported their men. She probably would have laughed at the idea, but she would have made a good candidate and, in another era, might have been one.

After Sugar's death, I continued as a partner in Syers-Pickle & Winn for another year, then left the agency to go into public relations on my own. Unfortunately, a few years later, Syers-Pickle & Winn failed.

Pickle Family Vine. Illustration by Dwain Kelley.

In the mid- and late fifties, I served as executive director for the State Democratic Executive Committee, and as one of Texas' three Employment Commissioners. Peggy lived with me and with Sugar's parents, Judge and Nora Critz, who opened their hearts and their big house on West Lynn, and provided a loving home for Peggy when I was on the road for days at a time. I owe Judge and Mrs. Critz a debt I can never repay, in this life or the next.

But if the family had supported me before, it rallied behind me big time in 1963, when I contemplated my first race for Congress. In the spring of 1963, Beryl and I had been married a little over two years. Beryl Bolton McCarroll Pickle was from East Texas; her parents, Tracy and Hazel Bolton were one of Jacksonville's pioneer families. Tracy was

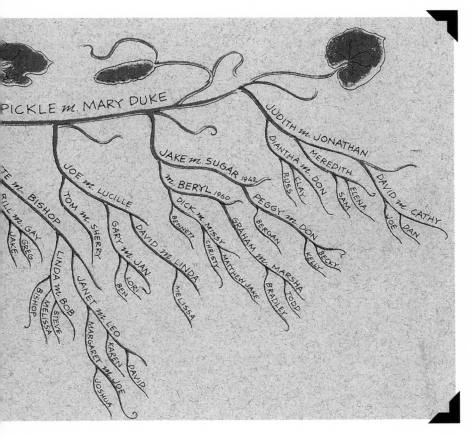

a conductor for Southern Pacific. He and Hazel raised five daughters: Barbara, Beryl, Frances, Lois, and Bunny.

Beryl's first husband, James Graham McCarroll, died suddenly in 1948 of a heart attack precipitated by high blood pressure. At age thirty-one, overnight she was a widow, as well as the mother of little boys, five years and thirteen months old. Beryl grieved and thought about the future. Then she took a deep breath and left her parents, sisters, and Jacksonville—in which she had lived her entire life—and moved to Austin so she could find a job that would support herself and the boys.

Beryl and I were introduced by mutual friends, Sue and Bill Stearns, at a party at their house in December 1953. We liked each other from the beginning, even though our first real date, several months later, was all wet. I took her to a party thrown by a couple of Texas legislators on a boat on Lake Austin. Beryl and I were sitting on a blanket on the bow of the boat when another boat went by at high speed, creating a rough wake. The bow of our boat heaved suddenly, and we were unceremoniously dumped into the lake. I didn't even know if Beryl could swim! Luckily, she could. We swam around to the stern and climbed back into the boat. Although her clothes and hair were soaked, she wasn't mad. That was the first time I learned Beryl was a good sport—and the first time she learned that keeping company with me meant lots of surprises.

We married in 1960. When I announced for Congress in 1963, Beryl had only recently quit her job as executive secretary to Texas Railroad Commissioner Bill Murray and, for the first time in over a decade, was enjoying being a stay-at-home mother, with me as breadwinner. Beryl's son Dick McCarroll was a sophomore at U.T., his brother Graham was a junior at Austin High, and Peggy was a senior at Austin High. Ours was the modest, typical two-parent household of three decades—and another world—ago.

That was when I dropped the bombshell: I was thinking about running for Congress. My good friend Homer Thornberry, who in 1963 had represented Texas' Tenth Congressional District for fourteen years, had just been appointed to a federal judgeship. After a life in politics, running other people's campaigns, I wanted the seat Thornberry was vacating.

At first Beryl couldn't believe it. Then she *did* believe it—and was against it. The logistics were daunting: how could we live in Washington with three kids in school in Texas? How could we support two residences? And what if—after quitting my job as Texas Employment Commissioner—*I lost the election?* How would we support the family then? She had a hundred questions, and I couldn't answer many of them.

I didn't try to talk her into it, although I admit I wanted it badly. I've always thought I owed my campaign, and subsequent election, to Nellie Connally, because Nellie *did* talk Beryl into it.

One day in the spring of 1963, Beryl, Nellie, John, and I drove down to the LBJ Ranch to discuss the race. The President, Lady Bird, John, and I climbed into a Lincoln and went for one of Johnson's legendary fast rides around the ranch. Nellie and Beryl stayed behind in a guest house to visit. Nellie, with decades of experience in the rough-and-tumble world of politics, advised Beryl to encourage me to run. As Beryl told me later, Nellie said, "If you say no, he *won't* run, but he'll always remember he had a shot and didn't take it because of you. It would be better to lose than not take the chance. If you lose, at least you'll lose together."

Beryl listened hard, thought it over, and gave her blessing. From that day on Beryl supported me 100 percent and sacrificed a lot to do it.

So that's when it all began. Thirty years ago campaigns emphasized how much the candidate—almost always male—was "a family man." During the summer and fall of 1963, Beryl, the kids, and I posed for campaign photos and television spots, wearing our Sunday best, more hair than we ever had again, and earnest expressions. We thought we were embarking on a great adventure, and we were. But at times over the next three decades, it was more like a great indenture.

If Beryl had any misconceptions about the glamour of politics, they were quickly dispelled when our first television commercial aired, an innocuous spot featuring the five of us wearing those Sunday clothes and earnest expressions, taped at KTBC-TV in Austin. That was when a woman called Beryl at home, to inform her that *she* didn't intend to vote for Jake, and that our television spot "was just like a farmer parading a prize cow so we can count the teats."

When I look at those photos and television spots now, I realize how far the family has come together. Those "children" now have children of their own. I was forty-nine in 1963—younger than any of my children are now.

Back then, the family thought that Jake, "J. J."—Daddy—was running for Congress. None of us realized we *all* were.

Everybody in the family has been affected in some way. Not long after I was elected, Graham and nephew John Atkin agreed to drive our Chrysler New Yorker—the infamous "White Shark"—from Austin to Washington, D.C. Somewhere in North Carolina they got a speeding ticket and, when pulled over, had a hard time convincing the highway policeman that the car, bearing Congressional license plates, wasn't stolen. They were finally released after paying a $100 fine—which was all the money they had. They drove the rest of the way to Washington without stopping or eating, arriving with barely fumes in the tank.

One election night in the 1980s, Travis County's vote counting machines broke down. As the precincts came in, votes had to be counted by hand. My stepson Dick heard a rumor about possible vote-counting irregularities and, without saying a word to anyone, drove to City Hall. He spent the night there, quietly watching the vote count, as he said, "just to make sure."

Over the years, my sister Judith and her husband, Jonathan Lancaster, campaign block-walked a hundred miles, rang as many doorbells, and faced down almost as many dogs hurling themselves at the screen as I did. Brother Joe drove six hours from Big Spring whenever I received an honor, big or small—and at age eighty-five, he's *still* doing it. Before her health failed, ninety-one-year-old sister Janice was right beside him. I think sister Jeanette, who died in 1953, would have been there, too.

For thirty-one years, I don't believe I ever looked at the audience at a major event and didn't see some of my family—often all of them.

My first grandchild, Bennett McCarroll, was also the first (but not last) grandchild to assemble Pickle pins, a painstaking, sweatshop process that required dipping the green pins in white ink to highlight "Jake," then soldering metal fasteners to the pins.

When my granddaughter Bergan Norris was fourteen, at that self-conscious age when dressing and fixing her hair consumed whole portions of her day, I took her to the Manchacha Fire Department's annual fish fry, and talked her into sitting in the dunking booth. And I personally threw the first baseball that dunked her! Bergan changed into a stranger's bathing suit in a tent, sat exposed on a trapeze, was dumped into and hauled out of a tank for an hour, and came home so wet she left a puddle on the floor of the car, but she did it happily because it was for me.

During a visit to Washington, grandchildren Christy McCarroll and Matthew Jake McCarroll climbed to the top of the U.S. Capitol with me. We walked in a 360-degree circle on the walkway above the dome as I proudly pointed out the sights of Washington, Virginia, and Maryland.

On Christmas Day, 1987, I wanted to make a dramatic arrival as Santa, so I borrowed an antique fire truck, and grandson Todd Mack, a volunteer fireman in West Lake Hills, spent Christmas morning driving me through West Austin.

In 1994, Bennett, my oldest grandchild, and Bradley McCarroll, my youngest grandchild, were in Washington for the Fourth of July—Beryl's and my last July Fourth in Washington. The family watched the fireworks on the Mall from the terrace outside Speaker Tom Foley's office in the Capitol.

After all those years, it was always a thrill to show off "my" Washington to my grandchildren. I hope when they are as old as I am, the memories will be as dear to them as they are to me now.

Beryl has sat through a thousand chicken and green pea dinners. And despite being basically a private person, she has filled in as speaker when I couldn't get to an event or was delayed, including a campaign rally in Austin in 1986, when my plane was stuck at the Dallas–Fort Worth airport. She stalled a crowd of two thousand at La Mansion Hotel by standing up and saying, "All over the country people may be asking 'Where's the beef?'" (in reference to a TV hamburger commercial popular at the time), "but I know that right now you're asking 'Where's the Pickle?'" She brought down the house.

During thirty-six years of marriage, Beryl's support and judgment have been my guiding star.

Beryl has also endured, at a thousand events where I received a lengthy and glowing introduction, being introduced almost as an afterthought, inevitably as "his lovely wife Beryl." It's become such a family joke that gifts to Beryl are sometimes tagged "To His Lovely Wife Beryl." The unsung hero of every Congressional career is the spouse. That was certainly true in my case.

During one of my 1980 campaigns, nephew Gary Pickle, who has a film production company in Austin and did many of my campaign spots, asked Peggy to dub a voice-over for a television commercial. She agreed, and spent the afternoon saying over and over into a mike: "This ad paid for by the J. J. 'Jake' Pickle for Re-election Committee."

At the end of the session, Peggy teased Gary by asking how big a check she could expect. Gary fired off a quip that has been repeated many times in our family. He said, "When you use the family talent, you pay the family rate!" Meaning zip. Zero, zilch, nada.

And speaking of family, let's not forget my staff. I've been accused of confusing family with staff and staff with family, and I guess I have. Certainly the good men and women who worked with me for over three decades became like family.

When I retired and closed up my Austin and Washington offices, it was traumatic because it broke up "the family." We must not be ready to say good-bye because we keep finding excuses to get together. For years I've joked, "You may leave the payroll, but you never leave the staff!" I'll keep calling on them as long as I live, and I hope they keep calling on me.

Over the years I have used the family talent. The family has sustained me, supported me, and set me straight. Sometimes I have asked the family to give by omission—by letting me go. I've been absent at birthdays, anniversaries, Mother's Day, graduations, and countless other milestones, because I was off being the Congressman—sometimes attending *other* people's birthdays, anniversaries, Mother's Days, and graduations.

The Fourth of July—when most families were cooking hamburgers and throwing frisbees to the dog—was a big working day for me. I could ride in three parades, attend a couple of rallies and a picnic or two, and have time left over to work the crowd waiting for the fireworks on Austin's Town Lake.

Milton's famous line "They also serve who only stand and wait" applies to political families—that talent pool that has kept me afloat all these years, and that I happily and shamelessly continue to exploit to this day. Paid at the family rate, of course!

Epilogue

Being Congressman was always a joy to me. Other than the long commute to and from Washington and, starting in the 1980s, the increasing partisanship of Congress, there was little I didn't like about being Congressman Pickle. Despite the stress, the long hours, and the lack of personal and financial privacy, members of Congress are given a truly fabulous perk: the opportunity to get things done. The votes we cast affect almost every American in some way—mostly, I hope, for the better.

The night I was elected, December 17, 1963—Beryl's and my third wedding anniversary—I felt I had been given an almost sacred trust to represent the people of the Tenth Congressional District. I never got over my awe of that trust. As the years went by, instead of working less, I sped up. Like Pop, who thought it was better to be dead than lazy, I understand the satisfying, seductive pleasure of work. All those years in Washington and Austin, Beryl and I never had an unlisted home phone number, because despite the occasional crank call or the 3 A.M. drunk with an ax to grind, I believe part of the job is being available and answerable to the people. That's what being a public servant means.

Every two years for three decades I campaigned as if my life depended upon it. In a way, it did. It was a life I loved, full of interesting people. And every weekend back in Texas, there were all those hands to shake! Just when things seemed perfect and (I admit it) a little dull, I got to campaign!

A hard campaign perked me up, made me sniff the wind, excited me. And although I complained about the long hours, the truth was that I loved tough campaigns. But they were hell on my staff and lonely for my family. My staff assigned campaign workers to me like horses, three per day; as each dropped off, a new one arrived. When people asked why I campaigned so hard, I said, "The political graveyards are full of the people who took it all for granted."

I never did. In thirty-one years in Congress I cast hundreds of hard votes, votes like the 1964 Civil Rights Bill that I agonized over for weeks—and a few votes I decided only at the last minute, when it came time to push the button. But I always tried to vote my conscience, tempered by the way I thought most of the people who sent me to Washington wanted me to vote.

My life has been given special purpose. Some men live to make money, or drink, chase women, collect art, excel at a sport, or pursue other things that give them pleasure. The thing I got hooked on was helping people. And I've had the pleasure of helping people by the thousands.

Serving in Congress was the greatest honor of my life.

Index